# WHAT
# MIGHT
# HAVE BEEN

## A CITY, A SCHOOL, AND A BOY RISE FROM THE ASHES

# WHAT MIGHT HAVE BEEN

## HAVE BEEN

A CITY, A SCHOOL, AND A BOY RISE FROM THE ASHES

BY

TONYBAZEN

What Might Have Been
Tony Bazen

ISBN - 978-163944903-3

*I dedicate this project to my family, my teachers,
my coaches, and my teammates.*

*You believed in me even when I didn't believe in myself.*

*Thank you for your love, encouragement, and prayers!*

# CONTENTS

# CHAPTER 1

## BUTTERFLIES NOW AND THEN

My heart beat wildly as I left the huddle and lined up at the wide receiver position that cold November night many years ago.

A little over a minute was all that remained on the scoreboard clock in our state playoff game. For the first time all season, our top-ranked and undefeated Southern High Spartans team was behind, and we were scrambling to score. Only 27 yards stood between us and victory.

The coach had called my play: flanker right post, belly left fake, bootleg right pass. Our quarterback, Randy Leathers, would fake a handoff to the left to our All-Everything fullback Darryl McGill, then Randy would roll right, and throw the ball to me in the right corner of the end zone. The play had worked perfectly all season.

If it worked again, our team would win the game. I would be the hero. Perhaps I would be carried off the field by jubilant teammates. Maybe one of the many college scouts there that night would notice me. Perhaps a college scholarship offer would come … maybe a pro career would follow.

As I tried to hear Randy bark out the snap count above the roar of the home crowd, I seriously thought my heart would explode through my chest. I can only recall a few times in my previous 17 years of existence when I had been this nervous.

I remember this same feeling on Valentine's Day of my fifth-grade year. To say that I lacked confidence growing up would be the understatement of the ages. When you are vertically challenged and shockingly slight of stature, like I was for most of my school days, self-assurance does not come easy. How small was I? I was the shortest person in my class all six years at Bethesda Elementary School, and as far as my weight was concerned, suffice it to say that a strong wind would have certainly carried me away. I don't recall my exact weight, but I remember so many times over the years of playing Pop Warner football for the Bethesda Cowboys that the officials during pregame weigh-ins would just smile and wave me on without making me climb onto the scales. I was not within shouting distance of the maximum weight limit to be eligible to play, and they seemed to think it humorous that a boy my size was on the team.

February 14th of 1976 was a special day because while playing for the Cowboys a few months earlier, I had fallen for one of the girls who cheered for our team, and I had finally decided on this day to let Janna Mitchell know my true feelings for her. Janna had beautiful black hair and dark skin–she was ethnically Chinese–and I thought she had to be the most beautiful person on planet Earth. I wanted to do something to let this exquisite creature know that she had captured my attention. I somehow scavenged enough money to buy her a gold necklace. Well, it was not genuine gold of course, but it glistened brightly when I spied it at the store. I could imagine Janna proudly wearing this priceless treasure around her perfect neck (yes, even her neck was perfect).

With impressive gift in hand, I tried to summon the courage to deliver the gift to this perfect girl. Janna lived close to the athletic park that was like a second home to me. Football in the fall, basketball in the winter, and baseball beginning in spring and spilling over into summer made Bethesda Athletic Park not only a landmark in the southern part of Durham, NC, but also a very familiar spot for me.

The plan was simple. After basketball practice ended, I would walk the short distance to Janna's house and give her THE GIFT. The gift that would certainly sweep her off her feet ... the gift that would guarantee her lifetime love and loyalty to me and only me ... the gift that would send shock waves throughout the entire school when it became public knowledge that Janna was my girl.

It was hard to concentrate on basketball when my thoughts were on the beautiful black-haired girl with the perfect everything. I ran numerous laps around the gym for missing layups that were normally automatic for me. I could not care less. All I wanted was for the final whistle to blow, signaling the end of practice, so I could put Operation Necklace into play.

Practice was finally over, and I sprinted to the restroom to make sure my shoulder-length black hair was in place. It is funny to reflect on how styles change over time. I grew up in the era of long hair and short shorts for boys. I was proud of my hair. Everyone needs something to make them different from the rest. To make them stand out in the crowd. For me, it was my thick, dark hair.

Satisfied with how my hair looked, I reached inside my gym bag to ensure that Janna's jewelry was still there. I exited the restroom and was spotted by Angela, my older sister. She was always tall for her age and had bright blond hair and fair skin. Angela was the oldest and was often tasked with taking care of Billy, the second-born, me who was the third in line, and Brenda, the baby of the family who everyone knew was daddy's favorite. Her motherly instinct kicked in when she saw me start towards the door of the gym. "Where are you going?"

I was too young to appreciate her concern. "It's none of your business. I'll be back in a few minutes."

"You know you shouldn't leave the gym with it dark outside already. I'm going to tell Momma on you if you do."

Why did I have to endure an overprotective big sister? Why did my mom have to work two jobs? Why was she never able to be there for us? Why was I always the last one to be picked up from practice? Why did I never have a parent there at any of my games to support me? Why did we have an ugly car? Why was I so tiny? Why couldn't I wear Levi's jeans and Nike tennis shoes? Why was my father a drunk? Why did he beat my mom?

So many questions. But for now, I needed to refocus on the important task at hand.

"Go ahead, you tattletale. I don't care. I'll be right back."

With that, I took off on the first step of my journey that would end at the doorstep of the world's most perfect girl.

# CHAPTER 2
## THE PATH TO THE PERFECT GIRL

I have always been a shy person. Maybe partly because growing up I always felt inferior to everyone else. The Bazens didn't seem to fit in anywhere. At least that was my take on things.

We were different. We were not originally from Durham. We had a weird last name, with less than 300 Bazen households in the entire country. Why couldn't I have been a Smith or a Jones or some normal name?

I remember momma's Tupperware party when I was five. Watching TV in our living room, I suddenly heard the loud voices of what sounded like thousands of women entering our home at the same time. I panicked, not wanting to face this group of strangers. It was too late to make a break for my bedroom, so I did the only thing that a rationally minded, painfully shy kid could do: I scurried behind the sofa. Believe it or not, I hid behind that sofa for over two hours, afraid to face these loud ladies.

With the Tupperware Terror as a backdrop, it's easy to understand the fear that gripped my heart as I got closer to Janna's house. What if Janna's dad opened the door? Maybe he was the prototypical protective Papa who would kidnap, torture, and slowly kill any boy stupid enough to try to talk to his daughter.

What if she had a Big Brother, and he answered the door? Maybe Janna's older brother was a bully who would love to beat my face to a bloody pulp for having the audacity to fall in love with his little sister. If she had a Big Brother, no doubt he would look Goliath-like in comparison to me, but when you were my size, everyone seemed enormous. Would I ever grow taller, or was I destined to always be the smallest person in my class?

I needed to face the facts. It was not her dear old Dad or Big Bad Brother that struck fear in my heart; it was the petite package of perfection named Janna that was causing me to hyperventilate. What would I say to her? What if she refused the gift? What if I froze with her standing in front of me and totally embarrassed myself?

My mouth became as dry as dust, and I began to feel physically sick. As I climbed onto the first step of her porch, I was sure I would throw up. What a great first impression! "Janna, I have a gift for you." Then vomit all over her. Or what if my heart actually beat right through my chest cavity and I collapsed right in front of her? Could 10-year-olds have heart attacks? I would surely be the first.

With my life now in danger, I had no choice but to make a quick about-face and sprint back to the gym. Angela was waiting inside, all too ready to lecture me on the dangers of traveling alone at night. As she began her discourse, she must have noticed the tears bursting forth from the corners of my eyes. I had done my best to hide these reminders that I was not a man, trying to mentally will my tear ducts to dry up. After all, my father said that only sissies cry.

"What's wrong, Tony?" My sister's concern seemed genuine. I turned quickly, pushed the gym door open, and stepped outside into the cold February evening, not wanting anyone else to hear my story. As soon as I was at a safe distance from the entrance to the gym, I revealed my dilemma. As I did, the floodgates opened, releasing a torrent of tears.

I poured my soul out to Angela, confessing my whole plot to steal Janna's heart with my Valentine's gift. I told her what had happened when I got to her door, detailing the panic I felt. "I'll go with you to give it to her," Angela volunteered. My heart filled with gratitude and I nodded my head, turning towards the path that I had to travel on my journey to Janna.

It's amazing how much bolder I felt with Big Sister walking beside me. I could do this. I could face my fear. I could complete this mission. No problem. Piece of cake.

As I took that first step up onto her porch, however, this paralyzing feeling overcame me, causing my legs to feel like jelly and all the breath to escape from my lungs. I couldn't breathe. The sudden pain that overtook me felt like a bullet to the chest. What was happening to me? It was Tupperware Terror Part II. I realized later that I suffered from an acute case of Can't. My infirmity was an Inferiority Complex. My sickness stemmed from shallow self-esteem. When all the chips of life were stacked together, I just didn't believe I measured up.

My paralysis left me glued to the first step, but Angela had not noticed and continued resolutely towards the door. I tried to tell her to stop. I wanted to scream, "Abort mission," but my mouth refused to muster even a single word. Big Sister reached up for the door knocker and loudly banged it twice against the ornate wooden door. "Clang, clang," it loudly echoed through the blustery night air.

The die had now been cast. I had been dragged across the Rubicon. There was no turning back. I heard steps coming from inside the house and approaching the door. The door handle slowly turned. As the door began to open, I summoned from somewhere deep within the strength to do something almost superhuman.

# CHAPTER 3

## SISTER SAVES THE DAY

Dick Fosbury is a name that only sports junkies like me would recall. My love for sports goes back even further than I can remember. As an infant, I'm told that my mother used sporting events on television as a type of pacifier. She said that watching the movement of the players, no matter the sport, fascinated me, and I could be content for literally hours while lying on a blanket in front of the television as various sporting events unfolded before my fascinated eyes.

I remember countless trips to the library while a student at Bethesda Elementary School. My "go-to" reads were always the Curious George series, but if all of these colorful books featuring the loveable ape George and his caring owner, "The Man in the Yellow Hat," were checked out (which was often the case because there were only seven books in the original series and our school library was very limited), my fallback plan was to find any sports stories I could get my hands on. My favorite sports were football (it wasn't until moving to China years later that I realized it was known globally as American football since another sport that only allowed the participants to use their feet had hijacked the name), basketball, and baseball. Not only did I voraciously read about the three sports, since these Big Three were the only ones offered in my area growing up, I also played them all.

By Grade 4, I had read every book even remotely related to my preferred sports and began to expand my sports horizons. It was around this time that I read about Fosbury and his amazing accomplishment in the high jump at the 1968 Summer Olympics in Mexico City. I think I related to this unassuming Mr. Average turned national hero more than the other Olympic legends whose stories adorned the pages of the books I devoured on a daily basis.

When Fosbury arrived in Mexico City, he was the most unlikely of unlikely stars. He was a gangly, white 21-year-old Civil Engineering student from Oregon State who looked more like a guy who would have a stethoscope rather than a gold medal swinging from his neck. Using his brains rather than his brawn, however, Fosbury concocted a method to clear the bar that dramatically revolutionized the high jump event. Using a back-layout approach that he dubbed the Fosbury Flop, he shocked the world by setting an Olympic and U.S. record in the event and occupied the highest spot on the medal platform, carving his glistening golden niche in sports history.

Who knows exactly all that crosses your mind when your life flashes before your eyes, but as the wooden front door of Janna's beautiful home slowly opened, perhaps I remembered Fosbury. Using physical resources that I didn't know I possessed, I sprang back-first á la Fosbury off the first step, over the railing, and into the bushes that were adjacent to the front porch. Maybe I could coin my leap for life as the Tony Tumble.

It was not deserving of a medal, but this Bazen back-first jump from Janna had temporarily given me refuge from the inner demons that kept screaming at me, "What are you doing, Tony? You live in a trailer, and she lives in a neatly kept brick house. She has the prototypical American *dream* family while you have a *dysfunctional* family. Her father is a respected business owner who is active in the community; your father struggles to keep a job because of his alcoholism. You are WAY out of your league, Tony."

Scratched and scarred but safe and sheltered now by the shrubs, I heard as Angela spoke to Janna's father and asked to speak with her. As she waited for Janna to appear at the door, Angela said in a LOUD whisper, "Tony, get up here right now! What are you doing? Janna is coming to the door."

Wild horses could not have pulled me from behind that bush. All I could say to Angela was a resolute, "No." Angela, now getting seriously annoyed, sternly said, "Tony, you better come here right now." Before I could respond, I heard the voice of an angel that drowned out the taunts of my inner demons and the anger of my sister. It was Janna.

"Hello, Angela. Good to see ya," the angelic voice from the top of the porch sang out. When I heard this voice from above, my breathing suddenly stopped, leaving me gasping for air. I'm certain that an EKG taken at this moment would have revealed a heart about to explode. What had I done? What was I thinking? How could I escape this mess of my own making? I mentioned that later in life, I ended up in China. I used to think that since China was on the opposite side of the planet, if you dug deep enough you would eventually burrow your way to Beijing. If I had a shovel with me at that moment, I would have started shoveling for Shanghai immediately.

Angela could have ruined me that night. She could have told Janna about her cowardly brother, who was too timid to give her the necklace himself. She could have outed me that night as I cowered behind the bushes. Instead, she did what she always did for Billy, Brenda, and me; she came to my rescue.

I could clearly see Angela as I crouched near the porch on that cold evening, and my heart almost stopped completely as she began to speak. "Sorry to bother you at night. Tony wanted to give you something for Valentine's Day, but he couldn't come tonight, so he asked me to bring it to you." This was a brilliant response, but there was one BIG problem. I still had the necklace. How could the necklace get from Point A (the coward crouching on the damp grass behind the bushes) to Point B (Big Sister) to Point C (the angel hovering above on the top of the porch)?

I mentioned that Angela was extremely tall for her age. Using her long legs, she took one step back and then moved over against the railing on the left side of the porch, positioning herself now on the second step. She then took her long arm and stealthily slipped it behind her back and reached it towards me as I cowered for cover. I saw her plan now, but could it actually work? Could I slip the box with the necklace through the bushes into Angela's waiting arms without being seen or heard?

I remember some conversation between Janna and Angela, but it is all a blur now. I had a laser focus on maneuvering the gift through the maze of branches into my sister's waiting hand without being noticed. Miraculously the mission was accomplished, and as quick as a flash my sister transferred the box from behind her back and presented it to Janna.

I could not see her clearly, but I heard the seraphic sound of her voice as she said, "This was so sweet of him to do. Please tell him, thank you." With that, the angelic Asian suddenly whirled, seemingly somewhat embarrassed by the whole situation, and disappeared inside her home.

The door now securely shut, my sister also turned and stepped down on the damp grass and turned toward her bush-hidden brother. As I stood up, the streetlight from the corner of the street illumined us, allowing our eyes to meet. When you are 10 years old, it's difficult to express all that is in your heart. The truth is, it is difficult to even comprehend all that you are feeling, much less express it.

Like countless other times during my childhood, Angela had saved the day. I wanted to say thank you. I wanted to express my love and appreciation, but not a single syllable escaped my mouth.

Looking back, I think what I wanted to say was simply, "I'm glad that you are my sister."

# CHAPTER 4

## OF RACE AND MEN

As I waited for the ball to be snapped, I thought about how lonely it felt to be at the flanker position at this particular moment. The ten-yard distance between my closest teammate, tight end Todd Wright (who later became somewhat like family when my baby sister married his younger brother) and I felt more like ten miles. I was closer to the opposing team than my own, as it had been drilled into us when we lined up at the flanker position precisely how far to be from the sideline.

Five yards from the enemy ... a million miles away from friendly forces ... I was supposed to get the ball with our undefeated season on the line. At the biggest moment in my life up to this point, I felt isolated ... alone ... surrounded by enemy forces ... no help in sight. Unfortunately, it was an all too familiar feeling.

I remember this feeling of isolation all the way back to kindergarten at East End Elementary school. We moved from Wilmington, my birthplace, to Durham when I was only two years old. For several years, we rented a small house on Farthing Street, an unassuming avenue tucked away near I-85 off Roxboro Street. This was 1968 Durham, and although I was far too young to understand it, a great transformation was taking place in this city and in many cities across the south in the good ole' U.S. of A.

The influence of Civil Rights icons like Dr. Martin Luther King, who spoke at Durham's all-black Hillside High School in 1956 and famously said, "If democracy is to live, segregation must die,"[1] helped usher in the winds of change, and in the year that I moved to Durham, some long-held racially divisive strongholds began to be blown over. The National Association for the Advancement of Colored People (NAACP), inspired by the life of Dr. King and spurred to action by his tragic assassination, sued the Durham County School System in 1968 in order to integrate its schools.

It's hard to fathom that during my lifetime, schools in America were segregated. In the same year that Baby Tony arrived in the "Bull City," the Durham County School Board finally charged forward with a plan to integrate the public schools. This plan, which mandated that all high schools and junior high schools would be integrated in the fall of 1969, was accepted by the Federal District Court in Greensboro. Because of space limitations and the need to purchase mobile units, the Federal District Judge gave an extra year to elementary schools to finally pull down the walls of color that divided the educational system in Durham. By 1970, the scourge of segregation was to be eradicated from our city.

Southern High School had been one of the last Durham County schools to integrate, and I can only imagine the angst that those first black students must have felt in 1969 when they stepped onto the campus of a school whose mascot was the Rebels and where Confederate flags were proudly waved at games and school events. This part of town in southern Durham was more rural, more hickish, and "Rednecks" abounded.

Thankfully, shortly after integration, the school mascot was officially changed from the Confederate flag-waving Rebels to the Spartans. When I arrived on campus in 1981 for my 10th-grade year (high schools were grades 10-12 in Durham schools at that time), however, some students at Southern still struggled to surrender long-held prejudices, and there was sometimes racial tension. Confederate flags were still sewn on the butts of faded jeans, T-shirts with mantras like "The South Will Rise Again" were a common sight, and the campus was divided into sections before school and during lunch. The Preps were stationed in the front vestibule of the school where they could proudly display their latest Lacoste apparel, jocks and cheerleaders occupied the hallway that led from the main building to the newer addition in the back, the Geeks were confined to the hallway near the computer labs, many African American students were stationed in another hallway somewhat separated from the main traffic flow, and the Rednecks always congregated in the breezeway between the old and the new building. The breezeway doubled as the smoking section, and to pass from one building to the next you had to pass through a cloud of smoke and walk past many black T-shirts clad, jeans-wearing, wallet-chained students whose thinking had been clouded by years of secondhand smoke from parental puffs of prejudice. Old habits and beliefs die hard, and this truth was visible each day at SHS.

When I started kindergarten in 1971, it was only the second year of integration in Durham. A strange phenomenon started to occur in the city of Durham, which also materialized all across America that for all intents and purposes kept the racial dynamic in the schools at almost status quo. In what became known as White Flight, many fair-skinned families in Durham, not wanting their children to attend school with children of color, moved out of the city where the majority of African Americans lived and took up residence in Durham County.

My family remained in our little home on Farthing Street longer than most white families in that area did, not because my parents had conquered the prejudices with which they had been indoctrinated growing up, but more so because of financial struggles. Brenda was born shortly after we moved to Durham, making her the fourth and last of the stairstep children in our family *(momma had her tubes tied after Brenda's birth … 4 and no more)*. Angela and Billy, not twins mind you, were both born in 1964, Angela in February, and Billy just sneaking into that same year on December 27th. I was born in May 1966, and then Brenda joined the Bazen Bunch in 1968.

Angela, as I mentioned earlier, was always tall for her age, fair-haired and fair-skinned, and very caring and thoughtful. Through the years she often took on the role of caretaker and protector for us, sometimes given more responsibility than was maybe best for someone her age. She was forced to grow up fast, but she seemed to relish the opportunities to help take care of her younger siblings when mom and dad were away at work. Angela enjoyed school (maybe it was a respite from all of her responsibilities at home), made good grades, and blossomed into a beautiful young lady. She was on the Homecoming Court and student council at Neal Junior High and was very popular at Southern.

Billy was also always tall for his age, nice looking, but like me, was also somewhat shy. We were opposites, however, in so many ways. I loved sports; he was never really that interested in any type of ball. I loved school and never missed a homework assignment; he never liked school, and homework was definitely not his thing. I liked R&B and rap; Billy loved heavy metal and even started his own hard rock band. I have limited electrical, mechanical, and carpentry skills; Billy could build a home from the ground up and at age 14, worked all summer to buy a '56 Chevy in which he rebuilt the engine himself. Momma used to correctly say that while I got all the book sense, Billy got all the common sense. There were many times as I got older that I wished I had even a tenth of the knowledge that Billy possessed about practical areas of life. Although quiet and often preferring to be alone, my brother cared deeply, as evidenced by his love and care for so many animals over the years.

When I stepped foot on campus at Southern in 1981, Billy and Angela were also there. This would be Billy's last hurrah at SHS as he dropped out later that year, deciding he would rather work than sit and listen to boring lectures at school. He eventually returned to get his GED, but for the moment he had his fill of homework, books, and teacher's dirty looks as the old kid's rhyme would say. By this time, Angela was a senior and at the height of her popularity. On any given morning during the '81-'82 school year, you would have found the trio of Bazens in three different sections of the school. Angela would be in the front of the school with the Preps, Billy (although he was not a smoker) would be in the breezeway with the "Rednecks," and I was trying to find a spot on the wall in the hallway with the Jocks.

Then there was Brenda, the prototypical baby of the family. Although we all knew that she was daddy's pet, and she could easily get us in trouble by saying we hit her, we all loved her. She was a kind soul who was liked by all who knew her. She would eventually become more like Billy in her dislike for school and love for hard rock music. When she eventually enrolled at Southern, she also dropped out after one year (although for different reasons), and she would also hang out in the breezeway whenever the opportunity arose since she was the only one of the four of us who became a smoker. We never realized how short our time with

Brenda would be, as she would be the first of the four Bazen children to die.

My mom, Rachel, had the unenviable task of taking care of this fearsome foursome, at the time all five years old or younger, while my dad drove a delivery truck for a local bread company. Times were tough then and only got tougher when momma's sister, Joanne, moved in with my cousin Mike, who was around the same age as me. Aunt JoJo was young, beautiful, and had a definite wild streak. She had fallen for a Hell's

Angel biker named Michael Karangalen, and he was not the fatherly type. After my cousin, Lil' Mike, was born, Big Mike took off, rarely to be seen again.

My mom had a heart as big as the ocean and always tried to help everyone, even if that meant sacrificing her own personal comfort. When Aunt JoJo and Lil' Mike needed a place to stay, our two-bedroom, one-bath bungalow on Farthing Street became home to eight people. Momma now was responsible for the care of five children, all under the age of six.

I never felt alone at home on Farthing Street since there were wall-to-wall people there. My first foray into public education, however, was quite a different story. East End Elementary, located at 515 Dowd Street, was started in 1909 as the third elementary school for African Americans in Durham. It had gained attention nationally in 1963 as calls for an end to school segregation were gaining steam, and a debate was scheduled between civil rights leader and Durham native Floyd McKissick, Chairman of The Congress of Racial Equality (CORE), and Nation of Islam leader Malcolm X. The debate took place on April 18th, after much controversy over a venue, and the central topic was integration of the races versus separatism. McKissick was a proponent for the former, and Malcolm X argued for the latter. Less than a week later, on April 24th, an arsonist set fire to East End Elementary, burning it to the ground. Citywide protests ignited when the dislocated students were refused the opportunity to temporarily attend a "white" school while their school was rebuilt.[2] These events were fuel to the integration fire that was sweeping Durham and the entire country, culminating in the 1969 Greensboro Federal Court ruling.

When I entered my kindergarten class in 1971 at the now rebuilt school, it was painfully obvious that integration, now in its second year, had yet to take hold. I found myself in a large class of well over 20 students, and I was the only white kid in class. Sometimes I remember it seemed cool, as I felt unique and certainly stood out. More often than not, however, the stares and comments made that year difficult. Back in the day, the term *"Cracker"* as a moniker for white people was in vogue. As the only "saltine" in the room, whenever the word was used *(and it seemed to be used often),* I always knew who the target of the verbal arrow was.

When I started kindergarten, my mom decided to join the workforce and landed a job at Western Auto. At one time, this auto supply and accessories company grew to over 1,200 stores nationwide but was bought out by Sears in 1985, who eventually sold the company to Advance Auto Parts. Aunt JoJo could stay home with Brenda, who daddy had affectionately named Lil' B, and Mike. Now the Big 'Uns, Angela, Billy, and me, were safely at school, and the Little 'Uns, Lil' Mike and Lil' B, were home under the care of JoJo. Momma, probably the hardest worker I have ever known, wanted to help out the family, so she journeyed out to Western Auto.

Steve was a mechanic at Western Auto. I don't remember his actual last name, but I realize now that Steve was his first name, not his last. Momma called him Black Steve for obvious reasons. While I didn't know his last name, I did know that he was one of the nicest men that I knew. His pearly white teeth always stood out on his ever-smiling face.

Billy and Angela rode the bus home from school each day, but momma decided that watching all five children at the same time would be too much for Aunt JoJo. Momma worked at a register at the store and could not leave when school was dismissed, so Steve volunteered to pick me up from school each day and bring me back to Western Auto. I would be there for around two hours each day as momma finished up her shift. I think she chose me because I was pretty self-sufficient and would not interfere with her work. I would choose an aisle each day and spend my time bringing all the products to the front, neatly arranging them in orderly stacks. My favorite was the battery aisle, and I could spend hours sorting and stacking these cylindrical toys, a type of poor man's Legos.

I never thought twice about Steve collecting me from school each day in his old blue pickup until one day at recess. Evidently, one of my classmates saw me get in the truck with Steve the day before and spread the word to the rest of the class. On the playground that morning, I was swinging on the playset when a choir of classmates formed a semicircle in front of me. Almost on cue, they began rhythmically chanting, "Tony's got a black daddy! Tony's got a black daddy!" I was trapped on the swing as they continued their taunts until finally, it slowed, and I jumped off, retreating to an isolated area on the playground away from the jeering crowd.

Looking back, I should have not been wounded by their words, as Steve was the type of man that any child should have been proud to call daddy. Something deep within me, however, signaled that this was not a good thing, and my classmates also considered a white boy having a black father as fertile soil for their verbal bullying. The world was not quite ready for this. My classmates were not ready for this. And I was not ready for this.

At the edge of the playground, safe for the moment from my tormentors, I stood alone. Although I had yet to join a team and knew little about football, already it appeared my position had been chosen. Flanker. Destined to stand alone.

# CHAPTER 5
## GREAT EXPECTATIONS

From my standing two-point stance, with my left leg forward and right leg back about two feet, I fixed my eyes on the ball and waited for the snap that would change my life. I did everything just as I had been drilled to do for years: from my distance from the tight end, to my alignment one yard behind the line of scrimmage, to the positioning of my feet, to the placement of my hands on my left knee. Everything was textbook and according to instructions. Well, almost everything.

At the flanker position, you were not to listen to the snap count but rather just watch the ball, since the distance from the center could make it difficult to hear the quarterback's cadence and lead you to jump offsides. All of my senses at that particular moment in time were heightened to a point that I had never experienced before and maybe never experienced since. My sense of touch caused me to note the tenseness of my hands as my right hand was placed on my left hand and both were resting upon my left leg near the kneecap. I could also feel the rain that had fallen all day and continued intermittently throughout the game. As this fateful last-ditch effort to win the game had begun a few minutes earlier, the rain had picked up, as if the gods decided to make things more difficult for us.

My sense of taste noticed the saltiness of my mouthpiece as I chewed on it nervously. My sense of smell seemed to detect the scent of freshly cut grass, as the field the day before had been perfectly manicured and looked pristine before the rain turned the gridiron into a muddy, gooey mess. My sight took in a thousand images all at once it seemed: the overflow crowd, with every seat filled and a ring of people pressed against the fence that surrounded the field; the Sky-5 helicopter from the local television station hovering above the stadium covering the marquee game of the night; and all the inhabitants of the field: the officials, the white-jersey clad opponent, and my teammates adorned in red jerseys and red pants. Although all of my senses were fully active, there was one, in particular, that had shifted into overdrive: my hearing.

Above the roar of the crowd, above the noise of the helicopter blades above, and above the shouts of the coaches from both sidelines as they yelled last-second instructions, I distinctly heard Randy, as he had done every football season for the last 10 years, confidently call out the snap count. *"Down,"* he commanded, and obediently all the linemen moved in rhythm from their two-point stance to a three-point stance, with their knees bent at a 45-degree angle, their left elbow on their left knee, and their right hand planted firmly in the turf like a flag on the moon. *"Set,"* Randy roared, and every muscle in my body tensed like a track runner waiting for the starter's gun, ready to explode off the ball.

Then finally, the climactic call, *"Hut One!"* As center Mike McClure snapped the ball into Randy's waiting hands, the play for which I had been preparing my entire life … the play that could change my future … the play that would alter the course of other's lives as well … had begun. Why was this play … this team … this season … so important?

The 1983 edition of the Southern High Spartans had been a long time in the making. Most of us had played together for many years, starting with Pop Warner football for the Bethesda Cowboys. Once in a generation in a town like Durham, a team will come along that is special. This was that team.

For years, Southern High School had been a football power but had never won a state championship. This team. This year. The title drought would finally end. This squad surely had a date with destiny.

"Big Al" Carson was the sports editor for the evening edition of the local newspaper, *The Durham Sun*. Carson was a rotund reporter who looked like he had never met a hamburger that he didn't like. He sported a thick beard during an era when facial hair wasn't fashionable. The '70s was a hairy decade, with boys proudly letting their locks grow long and many men's faces covered by beards or mustaches or both, especially in the early part of the decade as anti-authority voices expressed their dissent against the Vietnam War. The '80s ushered in change, perhaps in part because new President Ronald Reagan seemed strait-laced and, with his Trickle-Down economics policy seemingly fixing the nation's finances and the country no longer at war, there didn't seem to be as much to protest. By 1983, short hair and clean-shaven faces, other than the cheesy mustaches that all of us grew, were the norm for men. Obviously, Carson didn't get the memo.

Carson was not the guy you would select for your team in a pickup basketball game or the man who would adorn the cover of a GQ magazine, but he was a nice guy and a gifted writer. His preseason feature story on our team only served to heighten expectations. "There are some rumblings going on in the southeastern part of Durham County as the high school season nears. It sounds almost like a drumroll to some Southern High fans, who are expecting the most from their 1983 Spartans. So what is it all about? Well, now, it's like this. There was this really good junior high football team at Lowes Grove three years ago. They won their first six games, then lost a controversial decision in the rain at Hillsborough. This group made their way to Southern High as sophomores, where four went right to the Varsity, and the rest led the jayvee to a 9-1 record. Incidentally, that team lost its final game in the rain at Jordan, 14-13, after leading 13-0."[3]

Was "Big Al" a prophet? He emphasized how on two other occasions this group had suffered heartbreak in the rain, promising seasons ending in tears that mirrored the water falling from the sky. Surely fate would not allow another season to end like this.

There could be no doubt that Monty Davis felt the weight of these expectations. The man who had been nicknamed the Tasmanian Devil because of his short stature and fiery disposition ignored the advice of colleagues in the coaching community and took the reins as Head Coach at Southern High in 1968, taking the helm of a long-suffering program that had never had a winning record. By year two, he had the team on the winning track, a season highlighted by a win against crosstown rival Northern, his alma mater. He quickly established a perennial power, ultimately winning five Triangle

3-A Conference titles and making multiple playoff appearances. He was Coach of the Year in 1969, 1973, and 1979 and had been selected as an Assistant Coach in the Shrine Bowl in 1977.

Coach Davis had been the Savior for this football program, but anything less than a state title in his 16th year at the helm would precipitate a fall from grace. He had been following this special bunch of boys for years, attending games six years earlier when they suited up in the blue and gray for the Bethesda Cowboys. These boys were strong, they were fast, and they knew how to win.

Davis had been fortunate to coach some outstanding players, but only one of his former players had earned a full ride to a Division I college. The '83 squad was stocked with players with the potential to play at the next level, with seniors Darryl McGill, Kevin Sowell, Vincent "Cheeseburger" Ford, and the McClure twins (Mike and Mac) all Division I college prospects. Coach Davis beamed as he spoke with local reporters. "We've never had a situation like this before. As a matter of fact, if we've had one major college prospect a year, we've been fortunate. I expect there will be quite a few recruiters in the stands watching this coming year."[4]

The leader of the pack was Darryl, who stood five foot ten and a half inches, weighed 190 pounds and eventually rewrote the record books for SHS football. As a junior, he rushed for over 1,400 yards, setting a school record in the process, and was named the back of the year on the *Morning Herald's* All-Area team. Darryl was from a football family, and his dad, like Darryl, starred at fullback at Hillside High and North Carolina Central University. He also had a great uncle and a cousin who both played in the National Football League. "He has a chance to be really sought-after nationally," Davis said. "I've never had a back like him before. He can block, catch the ball, cut…he's just a stallion, a great player to watch."[5] College coaches around the nation had Darryl squarely on their radar, including traditional football powerhouse Oklahoma, Iowa State, and all the area Division I teams.

Paving the way for Darryl was left tackle Sowell, a six foot one, 232-pound monster who adopted the moniker "Friday the 13th" after the popular horror film. Kevin was All-Conference in 1982, and his reign of terror would surely continue in his senior season. College coaches at D-I programs like Georgia, Clemson, North Carolina, North Carolina State, and Wake Forest were salivating over the possibility of having Sowell sign on the dotted line to join their team, and some considered him to be the Spartans' best college prospect.

"Cheeseburger", all six foot three and 217 pounds of him, was given this lifelong nickname as a young boy because of his love for the popular McDonald's menu item. Vincent was a versatile athlete, but his forte was defense, where he was a terror on the line at the tackle position. He also played on the offensive line and even had the role of kicker. When he switched out his regular right cleat for his kicking shoe, he could rocket kickoffs deep into enemy territory, sometimes even reaching the end zone. If we wanted to attempt a field goal longer than 30-yards, he was our man. Cheeseburger was being actively recruited by Clemson and East Carolina, among others.

No discussion of the '83 team would be complete without the McClure twins, Mike (six foot one, 221 pounds) and Mac (six foot one, 224).

They had both garnered All-Conference honors the previous year, and it seemed as if they were born to play football. They both craved contact and could deliver devastating blows. Mike and Mac desired to play together at the next level, and N.C. State and East Carolina, among others, were offering package deals to secure the services of the brothers.

While this quintet garnered all the preseason hype, there were talented players at every position. Quarterback Randy Leathers had the physical tools to play at the next level, as his unique skill set and knowledge of his position were in high demand. We also had three ultra-talented juniors (Antuane Simmons, Todd Wright, and Arthur Wiggins) who started on our senior-dominated squad, and two of them actually ended up playing football at the next level while the other chose baseball over football in college. Counting these three juniors, we had nine players on this squad who possessed the skills to play college ball. After all these years of coaching and having only one player graduate and play Division I college football, Coach Davis now had the luxury of looking across a locker room littered with D-I prospects.

The major concern was the lack of depth, with the limited roster forcing many players to play both offense and defense. Carson again appeared to have some knowledge of the future. "If the Spartans lose one player to injury, it might mean that two positions are vacant. Certainly, quality without quantity is better than quantity without quality when it comes to football players. But it also means for the Spartans to live up to the expectations of many of their fans, they'll have to get the nod from Lady Luck."[6]

Other than limited numbers, you had to look hard to find flaws in this juggernaut. This team was special, and Coach knew it. So did everyone else.

One rival coach called us "a coach's dream team." The pressure only mounted on Davis with each new take in the local papers on the potential of this team.

- *"Coach Davis returns a senior class that may be his best ever"*
- *"Opposing coaches are talking about Davis having a shot at his first state title"*
- *"Coach Monte Davis makes no bones about this being his most talent-laded squad"*
- *"Spartans to be Cream of Triangle Crop"*
- *"Triangle Axis Hinges in '83 on Southern"*

Coach Davis did his best to put the brakes on the *"state championship or bust"* mentality that was gaining steam among the SHS faithful. "We have a depth problem. I'm concerned about it. I think we'll play well, but I don't think our fans ought to be disappointed with anything less than a 10-0 record."[7]

Davis was asked if he thought his team was invincible. Coach continued to try to temper expectations. "No. *If* we get in the playoffs, we'd have to play extremely well to advance." Truer words had never been spoken.

Carson ended his article like this, "So this is it. This is the year to pluck the fruit from the vine. With some extremely talented seniors, the Spartans are expected to have a banner season. Southern fans are thinking things like 10-0 and 11-0, 12-0, 13-0, 14-0 ... state championship. This team has a lot of potential. Only time will tell if this season is as special as Southern fans hope."[8]

# CHAPTER 6

# DYNAMITE COMES IN SMALL PACKAGES

The 1983 season officially kicked off with two-a-day practices on August 1st. For the football team at Southern, however, it was definitely a year-round commitment. Football players took weightlifting as a class year-round and only had a one-week break when school ended before "voluntary" summer workouts began. The term voluntary was somewhat humorous, as the penalty for missing weightlifting in June and July on Mondays, Wednesdays, and Fridays and conditioning on Tuesdays and Thursdays was so severe that in my three years on the team, I only remember one person who dared to defy the coaches and miss these workouts. This unfortunate soul didn't make it through the first week of two-a-days.

If you missed no more than two workouts during the summer, you would be in the 100% Club when official practices started, four or less you earned the 90% Club, six or less the 80% Club, and so on. At the end of an already physically draining practice, it was time to run wind sprints. These sprints covered the 53.3-yard width of the field and were ultracompetitive. The first day, the total of sprints would begin at five, and if you were in the 100% Club, you could go to the showers after this. If you were in the 90% Club, five additional sprints would be added for a total of 10; the 80% Club would have 10 added for a total of 15, and so forth. Those who failed to show up for voluntary summer workouts owed the coaches 30 wind sprints the very first day of August practices. With additional sprints added each successive day, it was obvious that you couldn't miss "voluntary" summer workouts and survive the brutal August heat when official practices began.

If there was anyone on our team who needed summer workouts, it was me, and I made the 100% Club all three years I played. All of my life I have felt like I was playing catch up, and this was certainly true physically. I was always either the smallest or one of the smallest on the team or in my class. I tried everything to increase my height and weight, even hanging from poles for long periods of time in hopes that it would make me taller and eating two raw eggs mixed in a glass of milk in an attempt to gain weight. Unfortunately, nothing seemed to work, and it seemed like my lot in life was to be little.

After I finished kindergarten, my family I guess did its version of White Flight and left the city, and we were able to rent a brick home on Jones Circle in the Bethesda Community in southern Durham. This was a big upgrade for us in many ways, as we moved from the cramped quarters on Farthing Street to a three-bedroom ranch with a carport, big backyard, bike trails galore, and even a gathering spot at a nearby creek called Big Rock. I have fond memories of living there for five years, and Bethesda seemed like a place where the Bazens belonged.

Bethesda had it all: a fire department, a convenience store, a big Baptist church, a reputable elementary school, and a very active Athletic Association with year-round sports, a new gymnasium, a football field, and several baseball fields. Bethesda Baptist Church sat on the corner of S. Miami Boulevard and Ellis Road, directly across from Bethesda Elementary School. After turning beside the church onto Ellis Road, you could reach Southern High School within five minutes.

Bethesda Athletic Park was a beehive of activity throughout the year, especially during football season. Out of the sports offered here, football was unquestionably the king. Given my lack of size and my family's lack of interest in sports, it was surprising that my brother Billy and I tried out for the Bethesda Cowboys when he was nine years old, and I was seven. I'm still not sure what precipitated this, but all these years later I can remember my mom loading us up in the car and driving us the short distance from Jones Circle to BAP. With our recent move to the area, perhaps mom thought that this would be a way for Billy and me to make friends as we continued to get acclimated to our new elementary school.

There was a large number interested in playing that year and cuts had to be made. When I made the age 7-8 team and Billy was cut from the 9-10 team, it set me on the path of a lifetime love for sports and caused Billy to lose interest in sports forever. I'm not sure what the coach saw in me that prompted him to give me a spot on the team; I was SO small, but I felt different when I put on my football equipment. I felt BIG … I felt strong … I felt secure … and wearing the blue and gray uniform that matched the other boys made me feel like I belonged.

After playing and coaching football for many years, I have observed that some people seem almost predestined to be players and some do not. Although size can unquestionably be an asset, I have seen Big Boys who seemed afraid of contact and undersized athletes who appeared predisposed to hit and hit hard. I was the latter, never afraid to hit even the biggest or the baddest. With my equipment on, I was transformed, and although exceedingly quiet and shy as a youth, my pads often spoke loudly.

A pivotal moment for me as a youth was during an Oklahoma drill when I was 10-years old. The drill took place in a small three to five-yard area, and it was undeniably a test of your manhood. In our version, one player would be the offensive lineman and one was the defensive lineman, and there would be a running back behind the offensive lineman who had to run the ball between the two tackling dummies placed on the ground.

The defense had to shed the block and tackle the ball carrier. It could be a brutal exercise, and it has been banned in many states today.

I always enjoyed this drill, no matter who the adversary would be that lined up across from me. I will never forget what happened one evening as Assistant Coach Worth Hill led the drill. I was lined up against a much bigger lineman and running back. When Coach Hill blew the whistle, I rammed my helmet into the helmet of the lineman, threw him to the side, and launched myself headfirst into the oncoming ball carrier. There was a loud, violent collision, and the bigger running back fell backward in a heap.

After these many years, I still vividly recall the war-whoops of my animated coach as he stopped the drill for a moment to celebrate my conquest of a much larger enemy. "WOOOOOOOH, WOOOOOOO! Did you see that? Did you see what he just did?" he yelled at the top of his lungs. Then he grabbed me by my facemask, looked me eyeball to eyeball, and uttered these life-changing words, "Son, if you were any bigger, I'd be afraid to line up in front of you!"

I had arrived, it seemed. I could do this. I was good at it, and I belonged. I was a Bethesda Cowboy, and being a Cowboy back then meant winning. In five years of wearing the blue and gray, losses were rare, and season-ending national tournaments or bowl games were the norm.

It was an exciting time, and life seemed good. A good school ... some good friends ... a good team. Yes, everything was good. Until the move.

# CHAPTER 7
## THE CIRCLE OF LIFE

Grade 6 was a memorable year for me, to say the least. On the plus side was my teacher, Mr. Gerald, who was both my first male and first African American teacher. He was a mountain of a man, at least he appeared to be larger than life, and I thought he hung the moon. He was a hero to me, with his engaging personality and witty sayings, and he became somewhat of a local hero when he helped disarm the school principal who brought a gun to a staff meeting, holding the entire group hostage before Mr. Gerald saved the day.

The big negative of that school year was our relocation from Bethesda to the Oak Grove community. My dad had for many years held jobs as a delivery man of various types of food, but he was able to secure his best paying job yet as a long-haul trucker. The job demanded that he would be away from home all week on these coast-to-coast expeditions, but the considerable increase in pay, coupled with my mom's stable employment at downtown Central Carolina Bank, motivated my parents to begin looking for a home of our own.

Their house-hunting led them to Pineview Drive, a sloping, dirt, dead-end road devoid of gravel that was marred by deep gullies. The owner of this off the beaten track of land had cleared some lots, allowing for single and double-wide trailers to be moved in for families desiring the

American dream to get their start. My parents chose the empty lot at the bottom of the hill on the right-hand side and then set off to shop for a mobile home. They found a large double-wide unit with three bedrooms, two baths, a formal living room, and a den. They hurriedly signed the papers, and before we kids understood the magnitude of the move we were about to make, we were boxing up our belongings on Jones Circle.

I'm not exactly sure when the realization hit the four Bazen children, but I'm sure many tears were shed when we finally understood that this move meant we would need to change schools. By this time, Angela and Billy were already attending Lowes Grove Junior High (in Durham County Schools at that time, junior high was grades 7-9), and Brenda and I were still at Bethesda. After much pleading, we convinced momma to make a way for us to stay at our current schools for at least one more year.

Momma gave the district our grandmother's address since she lived in the Bethesda/Lowes's Grove district, and for my sixth-grade year, mom had to scramble to make transportation arrangements to get four children to two different schools since the bus that passed by our neighborhood only took kids to classrooms that we had no desire to enter. This meant waking up earlier so that momma could load us all up in the family car, a horrible hoopdie that none of us wanted to be seen by our friends in. I remember often asking her to drop me off at Bethesda in an area where no one could see me exiting the car. Why couldn't my family have a nicer car? After attending Bethesda all these years and finally making it to sixth grade, the top of the totem pole, why was I facing so much upheaval?

When school ended, I got off the bus at a trailer park off Interstate 70 and waited at Grandma's until mom left work, made her way from downtown to southern Durham, came inside to help Grandma with something (she was paralyzed on her left side), and drove from our beloved Bethesda comfort zone to a scary new world. It was usually after 6:00 each night before we would arrive home, meaning that in the winter months, it had been dark for a long time already.

While I was glad that I could continue attending school at Bethesda, I was already feeling the effects of this move. I missed Jones Circle so much. I had spent about half of my life, over five years, in this familiar location. Now there would be no more hanging out with the neighborhood bicycle gang, no more BMX-style races on the many bike trails that surrounded our street, no more sitting on Big Rock by the creek, and no more visiting the house at the top of the road where an elderly couple operated a little Mom-and-Pop store where you could buy penny candy.

Separated from the Bethesda community also meant great difficulty in getting to and from practices, and by Grade 6, I was playing not only football but basketball and baseball as well. With dad away all week at his job and mom working late and then trying to gather all the children from the various locations, it was pretty common for her not to be there when practice ended. Looking back, I realize that it was not humanly possible to be in so many places simultaneously, but when you are eleven years old, all you can see is that many of the other boys had parents who watched their practices or at least were there waiting when it was over. Since I was often the last one to be picked up, this meant that the coach or some responsible adult had to be inconvenienced to stay late and wait with me. This mortified me to no end, and there would always be a knot in my stomach as I walked towards the parking lot after practice, hoping against hope that my ride would be waiting. I would often slip quietly into the cemetery next to the BAP gym and hide behind a big tombstone so that the coaches would assume I had been picked up already and not have to take time away from their families to wait with me.

As I waited for momma to arrive, I remember several chilly nights when she was later than normal. As I hid among the tombs, all the lights at the athletic park were shut off, and all the cars exited. I remember feeling cold. I remember feeling afraid as I crouched there in the dark. Waiting. Most of all, I remember feeling alone.

It's like my childhood … my innocence … all of this was left behind on Jones Circle. All of this was now gone, never to return.

Little did I know that things were about to go from bad to worse.

# CHAPTER 8
## PROBLEMS ON PINEVIEW DRIVE

Bill Bazen did not have an easy life. Growing up in Georgetown, South Carolina, near a little community appropriately named Bazen's Crossroads, he experienced an unbelievably painful tragedy when he was not quite 10-years old.

On October 20th, 1950, Bill had gotten into an argument with a neighborhood kid who was a little older and bigger, and evidently, the bully had hit him. When his father, Willie Bazen, got wind of this, his half-Cherokee Indian blood began to boil, and he loaded little Bill up in the car and drove down the street to confront the bully's dad.

Bill stayed in the front passenger seat of the car while his father marched right up to the front door of his adversary. A heated conversation ensued, ending with Willie saying his peace and then turning to leave. As he was about to enter the driver's side of the car, the bully's father snuck up behind him with a shotgun, aimed it at his head from close range, and squeezed the trigger. Bill watched in horror as his father's brains were splattered all over the front windshield, and his body fell a lifeless lump of clay to the ground. Willie Blease Bazen was only 34 years old.

Grieving son Bill never fully recovered from this. He blamed himself and sought an escape from his family, his home, his small town, and the constant reminders of that unspeakable incident. Believe it or not, somehow at age 15 he was able to secure a fake birth certificate and joined the military as nothing more and nothing less than a boy. His mother, Ann, agreed to let him sign up, and his birth certificate was conveniently "lost." Bill and his mother went to the courthouse in downtown Georgetown to secure a new document that

would "prove" that he was actually 18, old enough to heed Uncle Sam's plea of "We Want You." Somehow Ann finagled a new proof of identity for young Bill, and, in the process, his date of birth was changed from the actual date of October 27, 1940, to November 4, 1943. Bill, in essence, was "born again," possibly a precursor to his religious awakening that would take place many years later, and he kept his fictional date of discovering the world as his birthday for the remainder of his life.

Having the necessary documents to enlist, Bill chose the Army, opting to be a paratrooper with the 101st Airborne Division in Fort Campbell, Kentucky. He took his basic training there and eventually was assigned to Fort Benning, also in Kentucky. After three years of service and now actually 18 years old, he re-upped with the Army, and this Carolina boy was sent back closer home to Fort Bragg in Fayetteville, NC.

A boy thrust into a man's world, it wasn't long before he was drinking with the best of them, trying to drown the haunting thoughts of that awful October day in 1950. Like so many, Bill developed an addiction to alcohol that he battled most of the rest of his life. The demons of drink would haunt him almost until his grave.

Near the end of his first year stationed at Bragg, he took weekend leave with some buddies and traveled to Durham. On this fateful trip, he met

Rachel Lewis, a young lady who was also no stranger to heartache. Her mother ran an illegal liquor house and eventually gave birth to seven children from a host of fathers. The oldest of the seven, Barbara Jean, died from crib death at only six months old, leaving the second-born Rachel to help take care of the ones who would follow. Rachel had little recollection of two of her siblings, Danny and Frances, who were adopted out shortly after their birth and only reconnected with them many years later. The quartet that was left, Rachel and her three sisters Carolyn, Patricia, and Joanne, forged a tight bond that enabled them to survive a tough childhood.

No longer able to care for all four children, Rachel's mom sent Carolyn and her to an orphanage when she was only 10 years old. A few years later, Patricia and Joanne joined them there, and as the oldest, Rachel became the protector of her brood of sisters in this difficult place. At age 15, Rachel received a reprieve, getting a call to move to Durham to live with her Aunt Mozelle, where she stayed through graduation at Durham High School.

While a 17-year-old high school senior, she ran into a handsome soldier enjoying some R&R in the city and was immediately smitten by him. In a whirlwind romance, Bill and Rachel fell in love, and Bill proposed after getting word that he was being shipped to Germany to be stationed there. They wanted to be married before he left, so a date was set. Rachel moved back to Lillington, her birthplace, to await the tying of the knot for this madly in love couple.

November 4th, 1961 was a momentous day for Bill. Not only was this day his "birthday," early that morning he climbed aboard a plane and completed his 100th jump as a paratrooper, earning a new stripe and giving him the impetus to get a new tattoo recognizing this achievement. Later that afternoon, he took an even bigger plunge, traveling to Lillington in his finest Army dress uniform, standing before a Justice of the Peace, and exchanging vows with a beautiful young lady in a white wedding gown in the back of an old furniture store.

After serving his two-year stint in Germany, he decided he wanted no more of the transitory life of a soldier and went back home to Rachel. By this time, Bill's mother had remarried and moved to Wilmington, so the young couple moved to this coastal city to be near her and begin their own family. When I was born on May 14th, 1966, they now had three mouths to feed and decided to move to Durham in 1968 for more work opportunities.

I remember daddy drinking a lot when I was very young, but back then it always seemed like he would have what I called "good drunks." He would be happy, outgoing, the life of the party, and come out of his shell. He was not confident by nature, and it seemed that a fifth of liquor gave him courage. Progressively, his drinking problem got worse, and his behavior became more erratic. There was one time that he drank too much, was lying in bed, lit a cigarette, and fell asleep. The lit cigarette caught the bed on fire, badly burning my father's back, and he carried these scars with him for the rest of his life. Alcohol abuse has scorched the fabric of many families, and it threatened to badly burn any bliss the Bazen household might enjoy. By the time we moved from the rental home on Jones Circle to our own place on Pineview Drive, weekends at the Bazen household could be a frightening time, and I consistently spent many Saturdays and Sundays at my Aunt Carolyn and Uncle Owen's home.

After a week away from the family on the road as a long-haul trucker, my dad had a very familiar routine. He would arrive back in Durham on Friday afternoon just in time to pick Brenda and me up from school at Bethesda, and then we would drive the short distance from the school to the ABC store on Miami Boulevard. I wish this had been a school supply place, but in North Carolina at the time, ABC was short for Alcoholic Beverage Control. It was the only place in that part of town to buy liquor, and in my mind's eye, I still see my dad at the counter inside purchasing his weekly fifth of Canadian Mist. As a sixth-grade boy, I remember the knots I would feel deep inside, wondering what the weekend would hold in store.

Perhaps it was the memory of what happened to his father, maybe it was the pressure of paying for a new home and shortly afterward a new custom van and bright yellow boat, or possibly the strain of trying to raise four children, each with unique personalities and needs. Whatever the reason, my oft-drunk father began to experience far more "bad drunks" than good. These were the ones that led him to knock out the windows in our new double-wide, destroy new stuff that had been recently purchased, and get angry and curse the world. Sadly, these were the ones also that sometimes led him to hit my mother. Within a short time of our move, the police that patrolled the Oak Grove community knew our address by heart and became well-acquainted with our situation.

To make matters worse, momma was now working two jobs, leaving in the morning for her bank job, hustling to get the kids picked up from school and then back home safely, scrambling to cook a quick dinner (often Spam, boxed macaroni and cheese, and a can of Luck's Pinto Beans), and then speeding to her second job at 7-Eleven. I admire my mom, as looking back, the strength it took to often alone raise four children, keep food on the table, and try to give them a better life than she had growing up in the orphanage had to be superhuman.

As I reflect on my life from grades 6-9, I can see all the sacrifices my mom made ... all the things she did without ... just to try to make our lives happy and normal. I recall the motorcycles Billy and me got for Christmas when I was in the sixth grade, the tuxedo I cried for when it was time to go to the eighth-grade end-of-year dance, and the myriad of things that teenagers feel they must have to fit in meant that mom, in order to give us a normal life, could not live one herself. When I think of strength, when I think of determination, and when I picture love, selflessness, and sacrifice, I think of Rachel Bazen.

These years for me were a paradox. Growing up, I longed for the things that I saw my classmates have. I was convinced that the door to happiness was locked to me, and the key to unlock this door was some possession. But after we got the new van and the shiny boat, after Billy and I had motorcycles like most of the other neighborhood boys did, and when I was finally wearing Levi's jeans instead of Sear's Toughskins, I was the most unhappy that I had ever been. It has been said that "Children need your presence, not your presents." Truer words have never been spoken.

At a time when I needed a strong male role model, my dad was away on the road all week and then mentally AWOL on the weekends, often intoxicated and unable to provide the direction I needed. When I was needing the love and encouragement that only a mother can give, my mom was away working her fingers to the bones, trying to make us happy. As I entered the turbulent world of adolescence, with my body and voice changing, with all the insecurities common to this age magnified by my small stature, and with an inner voice crying out for help, I often felt alone.

# CHAPTER 9
## STARTING OVER

After a year of scrambling to get four kids to two different schools that were a good distance apart and then trying to arrange for them to get home from school, momma decided that a change was necessary. After moving to Pineview Drive, the school in our district was Neal Junior High. Although Angela and Billy were already attending Lowes Grove and all my friends from Bethesda would graduate from Grade 6 and go there as well, the three of us were transferred to Neal. Bethesda kids went to Lowes Grove; Oak Grove students went to Neal. I was about to become the young man without a country.

Even though by this time I had become accustomed to being alone, nothing in my past had prepared me for the transition to my new school. Imagine the trauma of stepping on a bus the first day of school and not seeing that familiar face with whom to sit. It seems like the bus ride lasts an eternity when you are sitting alone while everyone else already has a BFF. Picture arriving at school and entering a strange world with about 800 young teenagers, all trying to figure things out while at the same time trying to convince the world that they already have everything figured out. Couple this with the fact that I was undersized, underdressed as we still could not afford Lacoste or Polo, lacking confidence, and awkwardly shy.

The first week of school was a struggle for survival, with the goal being to avoid getting lost in this unfamiliar jungle while going from one class to the next and hoping against hope it seemed to find a friend. Enter Adam Finch. Adam rode the same bus as I did, and if you took a shortcut through the woods, we actually lived very close to each other. We both played football and seemed to have all the same classes, and by the second week, I mustered the courage to strike up a conversation with him. Little did I know that this pale-skinned kid that we nicknamed Casper (as in the Friendly Ghost) would become my best friend throughout high school and my roommate in college. In some ways, it seems as if he saved my life.

*Figure 1 Coach St. Pierre with the J.V. team. Like always, I was near my favorite teacher, wearing the #33 shirt.*

Two teachers in Grade 8 were also lifesavers, as their extra interest in me at a time when I desperately needed male role models was instrumental in my development. One was John Paul St. Pierre, who was my history teacher and also coached the jayvee football team and the baseball team. I thought Mr. St. Pierre had to be the coolest guy in the world with his outgoing personality, athletic ability, sporty car, and beautiful girlfriend.

I still remember his blond bombshell babe coming to baseball practice from time to time, donning her bikini and sunning herself on the hood of that red sports car. Rest assured that it was difficult for any of us to focus on baseball on those days.

Mr. St. Pierre's greatest attribute was that he truly cared. He took extra time to encourage me before and after class, and his investment wasn't wasted. He helped me believe in myself, and despite my size, made me the captain of the jayvee football team in Grade 8. I led the defensive huddles, called the plays, yelled encouragement to my teammates, and developed into a solid player. Our team was terrible, losing every game and only scoring 12 points the entire year, one of which was a touchdown run by me. I sometimes joke that I scored half of my team's points in the eighth grade, an unimpressive stat on a team as bad as we were. We also got crushed by Lowes Grove each year I was at Neal, and it was awkward playing against my former Bethesda teammates and friends. The experience, however, of playing both offense and defense and being a leader at Neal served me well later at Southern and, indeed, throughout my life. Mr. St. Pierre did more for me as a young man than he could ever have imagined, and I became a teacher and coach after graduation from college, mainly because of him.

I cannot mention my time at Neal without also referencing the impact of Jake Smith, my eighth-grade science teacher and basketball coach. Everything that Mr. St. Pierre was, Mr. Smith was not. St. Pierre was cool; Smith was a nerd. St. Pierre was athletic; Smith was six foot seven and could not dunk a basketball. St. Pierre had a sports car; Smith had a beater; St. Pierre had a model as a girlfriend; Smith … well, just say that the baseball team would not have been distracted if his wife was sunning on the hood of his hoopdie. They were different in almost every way, but the common denominator was that they both cared.

Mr. Smith took a special interest in me not as an athlete but as a student. I had always been a good student; he challenged me to be a great student. I'll never forget him asking me to remain after class one day, so he could speak with me. "Tony, you are an exceptional student," Smith said. "You lack confidence, however. You could be anything in life you choose to be. You can be a doctor or a lawyer. If you keep working hard, the sky is the limit in your life." Smith had no idea how things at home with my dad's drinking problem kept getting progressively worse or how often I felt discouraged or sometimes depressed as a young teenager. His words were like water to a thirsty soul, helping me to believe in myself and strive to achieve excellence. I'll never forget him inviting another student, Guy Bishop, and me to have a meal at his home with his wife and him at the end of the year. Mr. Smith truly cared.

Two different teachers. Two vastly different personalities. But they both made a big difference in my life. I have lost track of them both and for years have tried to hunt them down just to say thank you.

I missed my friends from Bethesda, but slowly I formed a circle of new friends. Looking back, going to Neal was good for me, forcing me out of my shell and giving me an opportunity to eventually become a leader. Lowes Grove was the newer, nicer, cooler school and had a lot more students. It was a big pond with many big fish. Neal was a little pond, and I went there as a little, unknown fish. When I left there for Southern after Grade 9, I was still small in stature but had become a big fish in this little pond, even being named Most Valuable Player of the jayvee football team in Grade 8 and elected President of the Student Council my last year there. The pain of starting over produced the fruit of emotional and social maturity. As much as I fought against this move to Neal as my time at Bethesda was ending, this push out of the nest was exactly what I needed to learn to fly.

Although I played basketball, baseball, and football at Neal, it was football that became my forte. Despite my lack of size, I enjoyed hitting and never shied away from contact. Perhaps there was pent-up anger within me that the violent collisions of the sport helped me to release. My dream as I journeyed through junior high was to play football for THE Southern Spartans.

When I was in the seventh grade, the Spartans had a talented team and made the playoffs. Adam and I hitched a ride from his mom and went to watch the big game at Southern High that Friday night. The game was tight throughout, but the Spartans came up short, ending their season. Adam and I raced from the bleachers to where the players were exiting the field and going back into the locker room, which was then inside the school. As we stood by the fence that separated the crowd from the players, we watched a despondent group of sweat-soaked warriors file past. In their uniforms, with their massive shoulder pads on, they looked humongous, larger than life.

I marveled at these gladiators. I envied them. I wanted to be a Spartan.

Boys, my age and some much younger, begged the players, since it was the last game, to give them a piece of their equipment. Many players ignored this bunch of begging boys, keeping their heads down and marching by without acknowledging our pleas. Some, however, stopped and took off various objects and tossed them over the fence as souvenirs for the awestruck adolescents. Arm pads, elbow pads, chin straps, and wristbands, all drenched in sweat and covered in mud, were among the items that made their way over the fence to be fought over by the crowd of boys. I missed out on all these treasures and thought I would leave empty-handed. I felt dejected until one straggling Spartan made eye contact with me, perhaps noticing my disappointment at being outfought for all the other items. He had already given away everything, it seemed, but then he noticed the mouthpiece dangling from the face mask of his helmet. With one powerful tug, he ripped it off his helmet and tossed it directly to me. I grabbed it, ignoring the fact that it had been in his mouth all game and was covered by his saliva. All that mattered was that I now owned a piece of Southern High football. I took it home, washed it, and placed it carefully in my memory box.

I have it still today.

# CHAPTER 10

## JOIN THE CLUB

My sophomore and junior years at Southern were extremely eventful, and many memories were made. Grade 10 had the excitement of reconnecting with old friends from Bethesda and playing on the jayvee football team. Of all the former friends from elementary school, it was Janna that I was looking forward to seeing the most. After Operation Necklace in Grade 5, she had been my "girlfriend" for a while, but I was so shy that I can rarely remember us talking. Back in the day, we would phrase a relationship as "we're going together" but you never went anywhere or "we're talking" but rarely did. I wondered what she looked like after three years. Did she still have the necklace? Would she even really remember me? Was it in the realm of possibility for us to get together and maybe this time actually go somewhere and even talk?

When I saw her, I quickly discovered two things. First of all, she was more beautiful now than before. Time had been good to her, and she was a downright head-turner. Her thick black hair, tanned skin, and perfect smile deserved a billboard on a main street. The second discovery about her was far less encouraging. Janna had a boyfriend, Craig, who was a senior. He was handsome, popular, and it was clear that my chances with Janna had gone from slim to none. Janna dated Craig throughout high school, and they eventually married. As far as relationships, I had to scratch this one off the list.

With Plan A now off the table, I turned my attention from females to football. When I stepped foot on campus that year, I stood five foot six and weighed all of 96 pounds. Definitely not the ideal physique for football. I remember when we worked out in the weight room, I could barely lift the 45-pound bar with no weight on either end. All the seniors got a good laugh watching this skinny sophomore struggling, arched back and all, to lift the empty bar. It was quite embarrassing, but I was determined to be a Spartans' football player and would not let some snickering seniors sidetrack my quest. I realize that I looked like anything but a high school football player, but I had resolved to play. Remarkably, I earned a starting spot on the defense that year at outside linebacker.

Our team that year terrorized the opposition, and we entered the last game of the season against the Jordan Falcons with an undefeated 9-0 record. We were the better team, but the torrential rain that blanketed the area that day made it difficult to move the ball, somewhat leveling the playing field. Despite this, we clung to a 13-7 lead with about a minute to go, when we faced fourth down from inside our own 10-yard line. I still remember Coach Davis running down from the stands, jumping the fence, and yelling for Coach Lillie (our jayvee coach) to take a safety instead of punting the ball. It made sense, as the safety would make the score 13-9, and we would get a free kick from our 20. The odds were that after kicking the ball, we would stop Jordan like we had all night and hold on for the win, culminating our perfect season. Disaster struck, however, when the wet ball was snapped to punter Tony Thomas, who lost his grip on it. Time stood still as the ball lay on the end zone grass, and a Falcon soared through the air, landed on the ball, and our undefeated season ended with a crushing 14-13 defeat.

So many tears were shed that cold, wet night, none more than from Tony Thomas, who blamed himself for this heartbreaking loss. We all loved Tony and did our best to encourage him and let him know that it wasn't his fault. It seemed like fate was angry with this group, rained upon our parade, and refused to let us end the season with a win. If we played Jordan 100 times, we would have won 99. We were that much better. Fate sent a fluke to snatch perfection away from us.

Grade 10 also ended with sadness for me. My dad's drinking and the accompanying erratic behavior continued to worsen. One incident in my tenth-grade year stands out in particular. My father had come home early one day from his job and had already downed one too many drinks. As normal, I came home from school and spread my books out on the coffee table, wanting to finish my homework before dinner. When my dad stumbled through the front door on this rainy fall afternoon, he was unfortunately having a "bad drunk." Even when drinking, he rarely spoke harshly to me, but today was different. "I'm tired of always seeing you with a book in your hands," he said with slurred speech. "You need to get up and take out the trash."

"Yes, sir. I'll do it now." My dad had taught us to always address people older than us with respect, and I never dared to question my father or speak disrespectfully to him, even if I strongly disagreed with his actions.

When I stood up to take out the trash, he grabbed my homework papers, ripped them in pieces, gathered all my textbooks, and threw them out the sliding glass door into the mud and rain. This was a harbinger to things completely falling apart at home, and one particularly violent episode during a drunken rage in June 1982 finally led my dad to move to South Carolina and never return. The next time I saw him would be on the Grand Strand in Myrtle Beach exactly two years later in June 1984 while on my Senior trip. This meeting lasted all of five minutes, ending with my dad handing me $100 for a graduation gift, saying goodbye, and getting into his tractor-trailer and driving away. It would be many years before I saw him again.

Before the beginning of football season in my junior year, Coach Davis called me to his office. "Tony, I want to talk to you about this season. You know that Bobby is a senior, and he was All-Conference last year (*he was referring to Bobby Larrabee who was a two-time All-Conference performer at Will linebacker*). If you play varsity this year, you may not get much playing time. If you decide to play jayvee again, you can play a lot and be a leader for us." I would have loved to be on the varsity as a junior, but more than anything, I wanted to play. Although I had grown to five foot nine and now weighed 120 pounds, I was still so small compared to the rest of my team. I chose to play jayvee, started on offense and defense, and we had a successful season with seven wins and only one loss.

Fast forward to August 1st, 1983. It was time for official practice to begin for my senior year. The summer workouts took on special meaning as I realized that this would be my last season as a high school football player. I had even earned the 500 Club T-shirt, not a big deal for many others but a huge accomplishment for me. We would find out the maximum weight we could lift on the bench press, squats, and clean and jerk. We would add these three together, and if the total was 500 pounds or more, you would be in the 500 Club, if the total was 750 pounds or higher, you would be a part of the 750 Club, and every so often there would be a person who would be a part of the 1,000 Club. I have seen Kevin Sowell squat over 600 pounds, which was more than the total of my three exercises, but I was still so proud to finally own proof of my entrance into the 500 Club.

It was this special shirt I had on when I saw her for the first time. The first two-a-day practice was over. We would arrive in the morning at 7:30 and have an intense practice until around 11:00. We would go home and rest, avoiding the hottest part of the day, and then return to school in the afternoon at 5:00 and practice until around 7:30. After the evening practice concluded, I showered, proudly slipped on my 500 Club T-shirt, and was walking towards the front of the school with Adam by my side. We took the long route to his car because we heard that the cheerleaders were practicing in the front vestibule of the school. As we walked through the long corridor that led from the breezeway to the front of the school, we could hear them long before we saw them. Both the varsity and junior varsity cheerleaders were practicing, and as we finally gained a visual on them, I spotted an unfamiliar face.

I turned to Adam and said, "Who is that girl?" pointing at Karen Rigsbee. She was perfectly petite, standing only about five foot tall, and was as thin as a Pringles on a diet. Like all the other cheerleaders that day, she had on red shorts and a white T-shirt, which perfectly framed her bronzed skin.

As we got closer, I noticed her short, brownish blonde hair, captivating eyes, and angelic face. "I don't know who she is," Adam responded. "She's cute."

As we were passing by, we spoke to some of the varsity cheerleaders, with Adam making special efforts to get the attention of Christie Baker, his longtime crush. "Hey Christie," Adam said. "Have you had a good summer?" They had some quick small talk about the beach trip many took when school ended and summer began, as many juniors were interlopers at Myrtle Beach for Senior week. I felt left out because I missed the trip to go to Boy's State, which looked good on my college transcript but felt so bad at the moment as I heard everyone talk about what a great time they had at Myrtle. Adam was also a gifted student and was part of the quintet from our school invited to this prestigious summer event on the campus of Wake Forest University that gave firsthand experience in how governments operate. Interestingly, four of the five who were invited were football players, as Vincent Ford, Tommy Upchurch, Adam, and I were given this opportunity, showing our team was not all brawn and no brains. Adam chose the beach over Boy's State, and when he finished talking with Christie, he took time to rub it in.

"I told you that you should have gone with us. We had a great time. You missed it, man."

I knew he was right, and I felt that hollow feeling that occurs when you are around others who shared a common experience that seemed so incredible, and they seemingly talk about it forever, but you missed out. A cloud of discouragement was trying to settle in over my head when it happened. I was looking again at Karen when she looked my way, and we made eye contact. She smiled at me. She had perfect white teeth (a big shout-out to her dad for paying for her braces) and when she smiled, her cheeks had the most magnificent dimples. I shyly smiled back, and we exited the school. I was hooked.

I looked at Adam and said confidently, "That girl's going to be my girlfriend."

"No way. I don't believe you have the guts to talk to her. Not going to happen." More than trying to discourage me, Adam was trying to challenge me to step up to the plate and take my swing rather than stay in the dugout dreaming of a home run. I didn't know at the time what genuine friendship was. Looking back over many years now, I've never had a truer, more loyal friend than Adam. He was that friend I could be myself with. The one I could share things with. He was a good guy.

"Just give me two weeks," I boasted, "and she will be mine." Despite the external confidence, inside I was far less certain. Had she actually noticed me, or did she just smile at everyone? Did I truly have a chance with her? What would be my strategy to get her attention?

I used the age-old method of securing information; I relayed information between friends. It went something like this. I got my best friend (Adam) to talk to Karen's best friend (Lee Small). "Hey, Lee. I think Tony is interested in your friend, Karen. He noticed her the other day and said he thought she was really pretty. Does she have a boyfriend? Do you think she would be interested in him?"

This backdoor approach was ingenious. It was a way to get information without putting your name and reputation completely on the line and without suffering personal embarrassment. As expected, Lee went directly to Karen and relayed Adam's message and soon returned with Karen's response.

"Karen had a boyfriend, but they broke up. She's single now. I think she would go out with Tony if he asked her." Adam took this message from Lee and made a beeline to me to share the good news.

"Hey man. I think she's interested. Ask her out."

Within days, she and I had gone on our first date, a movie at Northgate Mall, and Karen and her family became a big part of my life for the next two years. There had been other girls that I had liked in the past and who had liked me back, but this was in reality my first real relationship.

I was now officially not only in the 500 Club but also in the Girlfriend Club.

# CHAPTER 11

## A FEW GOOD MEN

Despite the success that Southern had enjoyed since Coach Davis' arrival, we didn't have an exceptionally large number of guys decide to play football. The basketball program had seen a resurgence in recent years, especially when Curtis Hunter took the court for the Spartans. Curtis was the first 5-star prospect ever at SHS, and he led Southern to never before reached heights during his time there. I remember when he was a senior (I was only a sophomore at the time) and coaches from across the country packed our gymnasium to watch him play. It was surreal to see coaching legends like Dean Smith from UNC, Coach Krzyzewski from Duke, and Jim Valvano from NCSU in the old gymnasium on our campus. Even after Curtis graduated, choosing to play for Dean at Carolina, our basketball program continued to dominate, and very few guys played both football and basketball. There were some basketball players who no doubt would have helped our football program, but basketball coach Larry Parrish kept them away from the gridiron. One, in particular, was Isaiah "Ike" Parrish, who was the best player on the SHS basketball team in '83-'84 and was also a state champion in the 110m high hurdles. Ike was perhaps the school's best athlete that year and would have been a major contributor to our football team.

Our baseball program had also enjoyed a renaissance under Coach Pete Shankle. He became a fixture in Southern sports and made the Spartans' baseball team a perennial state power. Shankle led the Spartans to two state runner-up finishes, eventually had the baseball field at Southern named after him, and was later inducted into the North Carolina High School Sports Hall of Fame. Although Coach Shankle was also the defensive coordinator and coached the defensive secondary for the football team, he couldn't persuade many of his "baseball boys" to play both sports. We sometimes called Coach Shankle "Pretty Boy" for his movie star good looks, as he resembled one of the heartthrobs of the 80s, Richard Gere. He was not lacking in confidence and rubbed some the wrong way, but he knew his football well, and he gave outstanding direction to our defensive backs.

The wrestling team was also experiencing success under Coach Keith Dodson. There were some football players who also wrestled, but likewise, there were many who wrestled but didn't play football, who could have helped us on the gridiron. The tension of having to lose weight to wrestle at lower weight classes and then desiring to gain weight for football was difficult to balance, so most chose one or the other. Coach Dodson also was one of the excellent coaching staff for the Spartans, in charge of our defensive tackles and middle linebackers.

With a limited pool of athletes with which to begin and a number of them only choosing to play one sport like basketball or baseball, our football team was lacking in numbers. The small number of players necessitated that many of us play on both sides of the ball that year, and the lack of depth did hurt us in some ways. The group of young men who comprised the '83 edition of SHS football was special indeed, and each of them contributed to the success we enjoyed.

One of the strengths of our team was our offensive line, perhaps one of the best in the history of the state. In his preseason breakdown of the team's strengths and weaknesses, Coach Davis pointed to the offensive line's size, strength, experience, and athletic ability.[9] Our football team rarely passed the ball, not because Randy was an inaccurate passer or that we had few good receivers, but simply because no one could stop our running attack. Opponents often knew what was coming, but our line was so big and strong that defenses were powerless to stop it. We normally employed a Power I Formation, with two Tight Ends and three running backs lined up behind our quarterback. Our offensive line was absolutely scary for opposing teams.

James Lillie was in charge of the offensive line, and he was a team favorite. Lillie, who had been an outstanding offensive guard at Hillside in the late 60s, was accurately described as the "cool, crazy coach." He was the only African American on the coaching staff, and while he connected with all players regardless of race, Lillie was able to relate especially well to our black teammates. Kevin Sowell pulled no punches when describing Coach Lillie's impact on him. "The only reason I didn't quit the team was because of him. He was one-of-a-kind. Always knew what to say. He was the best offensive coach I've ever known." Coach Lillie had been a part of the Spartan staff for some time, eventually also assuming the role of Head Coach of the jayvee squad. His alma mater was able to persuade him to take the reins of their program in 1985, so Lillie left Southern and led the downtrodden Hillside program to new heights, taking them to the playoffs six times in his 12 years there at the helm.

Coach Lillie was not a gambler, but he couldn't have been dealt a better hand than the seven men who formed our starting offensive line. It was not Seven-Card Stud he was handed, but Seven-Stud Line. Among this Sensational Seven were five college prospects and two who eventually played in the Shrine Bowl of the Carolinas, the annual All-Star game that pits the best high school players in North Carolina against the elite from South Carolina. You would be hard-pressed to find a better offensive line in the annals of NC prep football history than this one.

Starting at tight end on the right side was Todd, who I mentioned earlier. Todd was a junior, stood five foot ten, and tipped the scales at 195 pounds. Todd was relatively quiet, well-liked, and respected. He was deceptively quick and agile despite his lumbering look, even starring at fullback on the jayvee in Grade 10. He was what we would call "country strong." His body wasn't necessarily well-chiseled, but he was as strong as an ox. During his senior year, Todd was moved to the guard position and became one of the state's best interior linemen, earning a spot in the 1984 Shine Bowl game. He went to Elon College on scholarship but chose baseball over football. Todd was an all-around nice guy, typically smiling, and able to get along with almost anyone. It was no shock that he chose to become a firefighter after graduation, as he was the type who liked to help others. He later became the Morrisville Fire Chief and also served in city government. There was only one thing that I had against Todd: his brother Kenny.

Kenny was two years behind me, and his locker was actually located beneath mine in the field house, where we changed into our equipment for practice and games. After my sophomore year, Head Coach Monte Davis led a drive to build this much-needed facility, which would also contain an actual weight room. Up to that time, we worked out in a small space under the press box adjacent to the field. The money wasn't there to construct the field house, so coaches and players alike were challenged to buy and sell "bricks" upon which donors could have their name engraved as a permanent record of their contribution to the project. Players were also required to invest "sweat equity" in this project, and we spent many sweat-soaked summer days between my sophomore and junior seasons carrying cinder blocks and hauling wheelbarrow loads of concrete as this monument to Monte slowly took shape.

A state title team deserved championship-caliber facilities, and this field house, which would be ready to use my senior year, seemed to be the proper perk for the players who would wear the red and gray for the SHS Spartans team in 1983. After we occupied this new facility paid for, built by, and reserved for our football team, ground rules were established immediately. Policies were laid out, and a pecking order was established for the beautiful, shiny-red lockers. Upperclassmen got the top lockers while sophomores had to crouch to retrieve their equipment.

As I mentioned, Kenny was a sophomore (or a "slopmore" as they were also affectionately known), and he was assigned the locker directly below mine. His lot in life during Grade 10 was to bow beneath me as I used the easily accessible top locker above him. This must have been difficult for him since he was not really the bowing, pay your dues, wait-your-turn type. While I tolerated Kenny as a teammate, I never considered him a friend. If I would have had any idea that within a year, he would start dating my baby sister and later get her pregnant, I would have "accidentally" dropped my helmet on his head as he dressed below me or found a way to hurt him during practice.

During my freshman year of college, I received word that my sister was pregnant, and I returned home one weekend to find that Lil' B, the baby of the family, was having a baby of her own. I was angry... at Kenny... at Brenda ... at the world ... but mainly at myself. I hadn't been there for Brenda for the last three years. We used to be so close, as we were the two youngest children. For years we even wore the same size clothing, and she would often sneak into my bedroom and "borrow" my jeans or one of my shirts. I was angry because when Brenda perhaps needed me most as she entered the new world of high school, I was engrossed in my own world, so busy with my life that I had vacated hers. I had the same feeling in December 2017 as my baby sister lay dying of colon cancer in Durham, and I was half a world away in China, not there to help her as she was transitioning from this world to the next.

Brenda's transition to high school may have been smoother if I had been there to help, but I was a Southern Spartans football player then. I was BIG TIME, or so I thought. I not only had a school letter jacket like the other SHS athletes, but I also had a special shiny-red Spartan football jacket with my name embroidered on it specifically made for Southern's finest. Not only that, I had my spot on the wall on Jock Hall, and I couldn't be seen in the breezeway with Brenda and her bunch. If I could travel back in time, I would change this, as I have always loved my little sister, but you don't get many "do-overs" in life.

Now she was only 16 and married to a less than desirable individual, at least that was my feeling at the time. As my brother-in-law, however, my opinion of Kenny changed. I discovered he was actually a decent guy, and as a new member of our family, he always treated me with the utmost respect. Like all of us, I think, he battled some inner demons. His demons led him to use alcohol and drugs on a regular basis. The demons of others may not lead them to substance abuse but may take them down the path of depression, domestic violence, or other dysfunctional behavior. A lesson that I have learned as I have gotten older may sound like a cliché, but it is so true: we should not judge a man until we have walked a mile in his shoes. I grew to love Kenny and the two sons born to my sister and him.

Lined up beside Todd was right tackle Arthur Wiggins. Out of the 31 young men who were part of this team for the ages, only eight were students of color, and Arthur was one of them. The roughly 25% total of African Americans on the team mirrored the student population as well. Similar racial demographics would be present at the other two Durham County schools, Jordan and Northern, while the two city schools, Durham High and Hillside, were overwhelmingly black. Even though 14 years had now passed since the school system had been compelled to integrate, it was painfully clear that many in Durham were not ready for this transformation to take place. Some were willing to do anything, even move to another part of the city, to avoid "too much mixing of colors." Thankfully, on our team that year, the only colors that mattered were red and gray, our school colors. I never remember racist talk in our locker room or among our teammates. I never walked in their shoes, but I would dare say that most of our black teammates felt respected by teammates and coaches alike.

Arthur, like Todd, was also in Grade 11, and he shared other common traits with him as well. You rarely saw him when he wasn't smiling, his pearly whites brightening any room he entered. He was taller than Todd, standing an even six foot and weighing in at 194 pounds. His shoulder pads seemed somewhat oversized, and he looked much bigger than his weight would indicate. Perhaps the biggest challenge the coaching staff faced with Art was to make him meaner ... more vicious ... instill more of a killer instinct. He was such a nice guy that this took work, as it was not in his natural wheelhouse to attack. With some "tough love" coaching and by enrolling him in the School of Hard Knocks, the professors being the seniors, he eventually developed enough of a mean streak to strike fear in opposing defensive linemen. By his senior year, he was one of the area's best players and eventually played college football. How appropriate it was for Art to join the Navy after graduation and become a military lifer, transitioning seamlessly from protecting our quarterback to protecting our nation's back.

Duke Thomas, a short and stocky five foot six and 186 pounds, started at right guard. Duke and Tony Thomas were brothers, and both were well-liked by everyone on the team. Their parents were always willing to open their home to their sons' many friends, and many of us gathered at the Thomas home after graduation ceremonies ended for a dip in their large pool and all the beer you could drink. Duke smiled a lot, but he was a hitter, and he helped hold down his side of the line. Sadly, Duke left this world way too soon, dying suddenly in 2001. I was living in Gastonia, NC at the time, and I vividly recall getting the message from Tony that his brother had passed away. I was honored to speak at Duke's funeral service and thought about my own life that day. Although Duke was the first of the '83 team to depart this life, all of this team, including me, would one day follow. I was motivated that day to value each moment and to do what I could while I could, as we truly have no guarantee of tomorrow.

Bookending the left side of our line were the McClure brothers. At center was All-World Mike McClure and at tight end on the left side was the equally talented Mac McClure. These brothers were well known and feared throughout the Conference. Their father, an employee at Duke University, was a mountain of a man and taught his boys to be tough and hard-nosed. He bought boxing gloves and sparred with the twins until Mac got big enough to knock him out. He settled for nothing than the best athletically from them and pushed them hard. Maybe too hard at times.

If anyone was ever born to be a football player, it was Mike. He devoured the opposition. Offensively, he pancaked plenty of defensive tackles and linebackers, leaving them flat on their backs. Defensively, he ate quarterbacks and running backs for lunch. Mike was big and strong, and although he didn't run a blistering 40-yard dash, he was cat-quick. He anchored the middle of the line, and no one could penetrate the gaps on either side of him. He was an absolute beast! When he had the pads on, Mike also had a mean streak. I remember an incident in practice one day while we were having a live scrimmage. I ran the ball and was tackled by a group led by Mike. While I laid under the pile of men who had tackled me, I felt a sharp pain in my right calf muscle. Mike was pinching my leg under the pile. We were friends, and Mike meant no ill will towards me. On the field, however, the opponent was the enemy, even if the opponent was a teammate in a practice drill. It would take more than two hands to count the number of opponents that year that didn't get up from one of Mike's punishing hits. I often thought how glad I was not to have to line up across from him on Friday nights.

While identical in size, Mac had a different temperament than his twin brother. Mac was not as intense, although he could inflict just as much pain to opposing teams. To be hit by either of the McClure boys was not something you would soon forget, but Mac was more likely to help you up off the ground than Mike. Mac was switched from the interior of the offensive line to tight end for two major reasons. Coach Davis wanted to stack the left side of our line, especially the gap off-tackle where we ran our favorite play, belly-left, give-to-the-full. The reasoning was that most teams run to their right, so defenses put their best linemen on the left side of the ball. We flipped the script, loading up the left side with our biggest, baddest blockers. The second reason that Mac was moved to tight end was that he had good hands and better-than-average speed for his size. Coach Davis said this about Mac's athletic abilities. "He's deceptive. He looks like he's not running, but he runs a five-flat in the 40."[10]

At left guard was Tommy Upchurch, who was five foot eight and weighed 205 pounds. Upchurch, as everyone called him, was one of the many Bethesda boys on the team and was well-liked by us all. He was quiet, polite, and very respectful, so it seemed fitting after graduation when he enrolled in The Military College of South Carolina, aka The Citadel. His politeness off the field belied a fiery intensity on it. It was Upchurch who we would gather around as he led our pregame chant, and I'll never forget his red face as he screamed out the words that always fired us up. One teammate accurately described him as a "hellacious pulling guard that would knock your head off and was tough as nails." Upchurch was a model student and citizen and just basically a good guy. And like a good military defense system, he refused to let any enemy penetrate his line.

At left tackle was Kevin, an absolute terror on both offense and defense. He was a freakish athlete, with a rare combination of size, strength, and speed. I have personally never seen a stronger human being, as I have seen him squat so much weight that the bar was literally bending. He was so athletic that in ninth grade at Neal, the coaches moved him from offensive line to fullback. He kept his same number, and I'll never forget Big #77 in the green Neal jersey, literally dragging opponents downfield. Kevin also was a standout on the track team, showcasing his versatility.

There were rumors that some of our team made weekly trips behind the school building before games to light up a joint, or maybe worse, but Kevin definitely wasn't one of them. When he was interviewed for a feature article, he boldly spoke of his faith. "Despite his intimidating style of play, Sowell is not a typical football player. He finds the NFL drug problem disturbing and admits he has never had a taste of alcohol, much less tried any drugs. 'Oh, I go to parties and dances like everyone else,' he says. 'But I try to set an example, so people can look at me and say is it worth it or not. I don't think it's worth it. Anybody can live without that kind of stuff.' Sowell is also a unique player in another way. He is a member of the Fellowship of Christian Athletes and says even his love for football takes a back seat to his strong religious convictions. 'I'm not taking credit for anything I do out there [on the field],' he says. 'The credit goes to the Lord. Everything I do, weightlifting, anything, I do it for the Lord. He gave me this body, and I'm going to use it to my best potential.'"[11]

Kevin was the guy who could positively crush you, possibly knocking you unconscious as he did to a teammate one day in practice during a live scrimmage, then kneel beside you and pray for your recovery. He was truly a caring person who desired to help others, so he just made sense when he later moved to the Atlanta area and became a police officer, even becoming a part of the elite SWAT team in DeKalb County.

Our offensive line was the team's calling card, and we even had some depth there. Senior Brad Wall and junior David Davis could spell Mike at center if needed. Adam, Mike Wiggins, and Charles Lee were all seniors who were capable of stepping in at guard without our offense skipping a beat. Seniors Vincent Ford and Scott Lee along with juniors Steve Saraphis and Tony Harris provided quality depth at the tackle position. At tight end, senior Darren Dixon and junior David Andrews were ready to step in whenever called upon.

Coach Worth Hill, yes, the same one who had coached me at Bethesda, was responsible for our offensive backs. He had two sons, Worth Jr. and Brad, who matriculated to Southern, and he desired to be a part of their lives through football. Coach Hill made his living in law enforcement, rising to the rank of captain in the Durham Police Department and eventually being elected Sheriff in Durham County, a position he held for 18 years before his retirement in 2012. Charles Lee (no one ever just called him Charles) spoke of his love for Hill. "I would run through a brick wall for him. He gave me confidence and supported me even after high school." Jay Kapiko recalled him as a "great family man who always called us 'Sug' *(as in Sugar)* when we were 'pussyfooting' around." Coach Hill was thankful that he oversaw a stable of backs who did little pussyfooting around.

Randy was the starting quarterback, of course, but was ably backed up by Brent Ferrell and David Young, who also saw some time at running back. Darryl was the bell cow at fullback and was backed up by Spanky Boswell. Stanley Faison, Antuane Simmons, and I usually started at the other two running back positions, but there were many talented backs like Johnny Stanley, Steve McRay, Stacey Winston, and Jay who could carry the rock effectively as well.

Spanky and I shared a connection when his cousin Darryl married my oldest sister, Angela. There was a newspaper article early in the season that mentioned Spanky and gave a spot-on description of him. "Spanky Boswell isn't a classic runner like fullback Darryl McGill, but he rolls through the opposition like a bowling ball through ten-pins."[12] Spanky was also a guy that you wanted beside you in a brawl, as he never met a fight he didn't like, and would defend his friends and family to the death.

Stanley, sometimes called Stan or Stan The Man, was one of the school's best all-around athletes. He was a three-sport star, as Stanley was just as valuable to our basketball and track teams as he was to our football squad. He had scintillating speed, and his ability to line up at flanker and run deep routes would loosen defenses up for Darryl. Johnny may have spoken in a slow, southern drawl, but he was lightning fast, the swiftest white boy at the school. Steve was a little guy like me, and was nicknamed Spark Plug because of his scrappy, gritty, never-say-die mentality. He was paralyzed in 2016 by a gunshot to the back when someone attempted to rob him, and the injuries he sustained left him confined to a wheelchair. It was no surprise when Steve took life's lemons and made lemonade, becoming active in wheelchair basketball and golf and later running his own business. As the saying goes, you can't keep a good man down.

As we practiced during the preseason, there was no doubt that we had an outstanding offense. We had no idea, however, that this group would become the state's best.

Before the season started, Coach Davis had some concerns on the defensive side of the ball. "As you have looked through our strengths and weaknesses, you probably have realized that our offense is our strong suit, and our defense has a lot of question marks." [13] As the year progressed, the defense transformed from a question mark into an exclamation point.

The middle of our defense was the Great Wall, with both starting defensive tackles, Mike and Cheeseburger, and well as both middle linebackers, Kevin and Mac, being major college prospects. No one could run up the middle on us. Mike, Mac, and Kevin were two-way starters, but Cheeseburger focused mainly on defense, and he was almost impossible to block. The Big Cheese didn't so much run as he glided, his long legs gobbling up turf effortlessly, making his path to opposing quarterbacks seem like a simple two-step process. Although a terror on defense, Vincent was a very thoughtful, intelligent, well-spoken, caring individual who always had your back both on the field and off. He was that "once a friend, always a friend" guy who people wanted in their corner. For many years in Charlotte, Vincent "Cheeseburger" Ford was a banker who stood in the corner with multitudes of people, helping them through life's difficult times.

Coach Dodson was responsible for this group, and beneath his loud and gruff manner was a heart of gold. He was Paul Bunyan in coaching shorts and always sported a thick mustache. Tony Thomas was right when he described Dodson as a "great man who made football fun." He had a great sense of humor, able to snap off hilarious one-liners at the drop of a hat. Coach Dodson was intense and very serious about helping his players reach their potential, but he also helped keep things light.

Many players recall one hot summer day when Coach Dodson and Randy engaged in a wager involving a grasshopper. Our practice field was loaded with locusts, and when Coach Dodson told us about his survival training in the military, Randy dared him to eat one of the insects that surrounded us. Coach said that he would eat half of the grasshopper if Randy ate the other half. The deal was struck, a big, juicy critter was obtained, and Coach went first. He chomped down on the back end of the grasshopper, ripping its body in half, and gave the other half to Randy, who devoured the smaller half. Within minutes, our military-trained coach was vomiting in his office, sick as a dog. Once we knew he was ok, we all had a good laugh. Incidents like this, as insignificant as they seem, created bonds and helped us endure the difficult preseason practices.

With the middle of our defense like an impenetrable steel wall, the question marks were on the outside as both defensive ends and both outside linebackers would be new starters. Bob Bickel, a quiet, unassuming coach compared to the rest of the staff, was tasked with whipping this group into shape. Since he was my position coach on defense, I thought I knew him pretty well but really had no idea of what an elite athlete he had been. Coach Bickel was a two-sport star at Duke University from 1948 to 1951. In football, he was named team MVP his senior year, excelling both as a running back and as a punter. He was even drafted by the New York Giants in 1952 and eventually played one year of pro football in Canada. Coach Bickel also earned All-American honors in lacrosse, demonstrating his amazing athletic prowess.

I had heard that Coach Bickel played for Duke as a punter but never pictured him as a star athlete. He was never one to bring attention to himself, instead just focused on investing in his players. Perhaps the fact that he was much older than the other coaches and looked his age (he was 55 in 1983) made it harder for some to relate to him, but those of us whom he directly coached knew he was a very approachable leader and sincerely cared. Right defensive end Charles Lee said that Bickel was the "first coach I ever had that showed confidence in me, fought for me, and stood up for me." Antoine played at left defensive end and never forgot the impact the Duke legend had on his football career. "I'm really grateful to Coach Bickel for teaching me great technique and trusting my talent. He once said, 'Take all the thinking out of it and play instinctually and you'll be fine, Antuane.' When he told me that, it took my game to another level." Coach Bickel also believed in giving chances to undersized players like Stacey, Steve, and me to play Will linebacker, which was more like a strong safety. He did not look at the size of the body; he focused on the size of the heart.

Coach Bickel entered the season needing to find four new starters to defend the edges, and he had to be pleased with the players he coached up and sent onto the field each week. Charles Lee and Antuane started at defensive ends, and both had tremendous years. Because he was surrounded by all of those senior studs on our squad, Antuane somewhat flew under the radar in 1983. He was the only junior to start on defense, and although he didn't get a lot of press that year, he was one of our best defenders. The following year he would get his due, being selected first-team All-Conference at both defensive end and tight end, first-team All-Area at defensive end, second-team All-Area at tight end, and honorable mention All-State at tight end. Antuane played in the secondary at Division I East Carolina when he graduated from SHS.

As good of a player as he was, he was an even better person. Always smiling, always upbeat, and that person who made the people around him better, Antuane was a devout Christian and not ashamed of it. He never drank or did drugs, but he was not that guy who stood in judgment of others who did. He later rose to First Sergeant as a member of the North Carolina Army National Guard for over 33 years, and I thought about how lucky all those guys in his unit were to serve alongside a quality human being like Antuane Simmons.

Charles Lee, Adam, and I hung out a lot. This trio could usually be found at McDonald's each Friday afternoon for our pregame meal, and we enjoyed countless good times together. Charles stepped into the starting position at right defensive end and had a great senior year, consistently keeping contain on his side and putting good pressure on the quarterback on pass plays. Charles was never one afraid of challenges, as he had the courage when he was only a sophomore to ask out a varsity cheerleader, a senior at that. Joanne Overcash said "Yes," and although their relationship ended for a time when she graduated from Southern, she eventually "came around" as Charles would later say, and they were married after he graduated from UNC-Chapel Hill.

You can often discover much about a man's character by examining what he decides to do with his life. Charles devoted his time to public service, retiring after over 30 years as a lieutenant for the North Carolina State Highway Patrol. Charles was also a prime mover annually promoting the Special Olympics, volunteering for years as the Highway Patrol's Law Enforcement Torch Run Coordinator. At defensive end, he came charging in from the edge; in life, he led from out front, a torchbearer for making a difference.

Tommy Upchurch and I started at the outside linebacker positions, with Brad and Stacey being very capable backups. Stacey was my boy, one of my best friends on the team, who was just fun to be around. Adjectives used to describe him were "small, tough, and scrappy," and Stacey was truly not afraid of anything. Playing the same positions on offense and defense as undersized athletes brought us together in Grade 10, and our friendship grew stronger each successive year. When asked years later about our unique bond, he responded, "Our friendship meant the world to me. We were underdogs, but we stood together."

Coach Shankle led the football team at Lowes Grove before coming to Southern, so he was very familiar with many of the players already. Jay had played for Shankle in junior high and had a deep appreciation for him, describing Shankle as "a cocky SOB, which is what you had to be to play defensive back for him." Shankle bought towels for all the defensive backs embroidered with the word "STICK," a double meaning challenging the secondary to stick to the receivers closely and also to "stick" ball carriers, which meant to hit them hard. Our secondary did both all year, shutting down opponents' passing attacks and delivering punishing blows to running backs.

Brent was our only returner with varsity experience and had an outstanding season, becoming one of the areas' top safeties. He had a real nose for the football and led our team in interceptions. Darryl and Stanley alternated at one cornerback position, and Jay started at the other. Jay, ethnically Hawaiian, was another good friend at SHS. We both played for the Bethesda Cowboys and had similar personalities. If a running back penetrated our first line of defense, Jay was there for run support, making key stops throughout the year. He was really an unsung hero on our defense, quietly having a super season. He became a teacher and coach after graduation, and many of his former students in his over 30 years in education would label him as their favorite teacher.

Opposing teams would enter the battle with far more soldiers at their disposal. We would dress only 31. We played different positions on the field then, and in the future, we would also hold many different positions in life.

A fire chief. A teacher. A highway patrolman. A Navy lifer. A banker. A police officer. An Army vet. 31 strong. A few good men.

# CHAPTER 12

## TWO STEPS BEHIND

Randy Steven Leathers was born on May 12th, 1966. This is significant because I also was born that same year in that same month, only two days later on May 14th. It seemed like from the very start, I would have to play catch up when it came to Randy. I was destined to be two steps behind.

Randy and I were classmates at Bethesda almost every year. He was the boy I think all the other boys, including me, wanted to be. He was the Tom Brady of our era and our town: good-looking, the long-time quarterback of a successful team, a beautiful girl by his side always, well-spoken, and popular. Randy, like Brady, even wore #12. He excelled at everything he attempted, starring at shortstop in baseball and playing point guard in basketball along with his cemented role at quarterback. He played all the glamour positions in the Big 3 sports in our area. Everyone knew him, and if we had been honest, we all envied him to some degree. Randy, it seemed, was perfect.

Randy was also from a wonderful family. His father, Norman Leathers, was well known in the Durham community. He was Fire Safety Director for Duke Medical Center, and his smiling face was a fixture in the Bethesda family. Randy's mother, Lillian, was also an amazing lady.

She was very active in Bethesda athletics, often taking her turn in the concession booth and very involved in the many end-of-the-season trips that our teams would take. Mrs. Leathers was a Sunday School teacher at Bethesda Baptist and over the years taught many of the future Southern High football players and cheerleaders. Randy's older brother Mickey was also a familiar face in the Bethesda community and was very well-respected. The Leathers were just good people.

Mr. Leathers had been an assistant football coach at Durham High and had also coached Pop Warner football in the area. In addition, he coached baseball and basketball, and I had the privilege when I was eleven years old to be drafted by him one year to play on his basketball team. This was a powerful team that featured my future Southern football teammates Tommy Upchurch, Brent Ferrell, the McClure twins, and, of course, Randy. A highlight for me that year occurred after one of our basketball games, as I was invited to spend the night at the Leathers' home. I remember that their home was immaculate, and I was completely in awe of the privilege of staying overnight at the home of the classmate and family that I admired so much.

I think I had a perplexing love/hate relationship with Randy. On the one hand, I idolized him and wanted to be just like him. I would try to emulate his confidence, the swagger with which he walked, and the smoothness with which he talked. I sometimes struggled with getting my words out, even to the point of being referred to speech therapy classes in Grade 5. Randy was Mr. Suave, even when talking to girls, the group with whom I particularly struggled to communicate. I remember Randy taking home numerous ribbons on Field Days at Bethesda, as he was faster and just plain better than everyone else athletically. My only Field Day claim to fame during those Bethesda years was being virtually unbeatable in the Limbo, as my short stature and flexibility enabled me to easily make it under the lowest bar. Randy was Mr. Perfect, with the perfect family and the perfect smile. I undeniably looked up to him.

On the other hand, I envied him and wondered why he was born with the silver spoon. Perhaps Randy was the one I had in mind the night I knelt in front of the wooden sign in front of Freedom Baptist Church, about a half-mile from our double-wide. I had run the whole way from home the night my dad had a "bad drunk" and pulled a gun out, causing us to flee in fear. After this sprint to the church, I collapsed in front of the sign, partially from physical exhaustion and partly from emotional fatigue, as the events at home were becoming a common occurrence. I poured out my soul to a God I had yet to come to know, and through my bitter tears, I questioned Him as to why others had it so easy, growing up in "normal" families, and my family had such turmoil. As I have gotten older, I have realized that each family has its dysfunctions, and the proverbial perfect family is a myth. That night, however, I longed for what I thought others had, and I thought it unfair for Randy to have so much.

Randy was far more than an elementary school Field Day legend; he was a very versatile athlete. Although he was the star quarterback for all those years at Bethesda, Lowes Grove, and then Southern, baseball was perhaps his best sport. After graduating from Southern, he went to Cullowhee, NC and walked on to both the football and baseball teams at

Western Carolina. Randy was on track to get a baseball scholarship if not for one problem: he didn't attend class. Randy had dedicated parents and dynamic potential, but he had a definite problem. It was a problem that surfaced in the lives of so many across America during this time as illegal drugs ran rampant on high school campuses and crack cocaine invaded our land. It was the same struggle that many students in Durham's high schools were facing -drug addiction.

It would be nearly impossible to get an accurate count of how many students in my graduating class at least experimented with illegal drugs. This was a time in life when so many youths were searching for something, testing boundaries, and pushing the limits. The new kid on the block in the drug neighborhood, crack cocaine, was accessible, affordable, and highly addictive. Around the time the graduating class of '84 was moving their tassels from one side of their caps to the other, crack had many in its clutches. "The biggest surge in the use of the drug occurred during the "crack epidemic," between 1984 and 1990 when the drug spread across American cities. The crack epidemic dramatically increased the number of Americans addicted to cocaine. In 1985, the number of people who admitted using cocaine on a routine basis increased from 4.2 million to 5.8 million."[14]

The demons of drugs that had surfaced in his life all the way back to ninth grade grew more powerful, and he left the mountains of North Carolina and moved to Fayetteville to play baseball at Methodist University. Cocaine is a cruel taskmaster, and when Randy couldn't break its shackles, he decided to go to rehab, thus ending his opportunity to play college sports. He later wound up on the wrong side of the law and was given a 30-year prison sentence in North Carolina. After serving 10 years of this sentence, he was released and ran afoul of the law again, this time being incarcerated in Colorado. Drugs will take you further than you want to go, keep you longer than you want to stay, and cost you more than you want to pay. Randy would attest to this.

I heard the rumors of Randy's drug use in high school, but when I thought of drugs, I only thought of marijuana. I did not realize that harder, far more destructive drugs had made their way onto our campus and that our star quarterback was struggling with addiction. And sadly, addiction doesn't just affect the addict; it impacts all those in his life.

By our senior year, I had not caught Randy, but I was nipping at his heels. Whereas academically there was a time we were neck and neck, I finally surpassed him and moved near the top of our class. I was also growing physically, still underweight at only 139 pounds but now at five foot ten a whole inch taller than my friendly foe. No, I wasn't the quarterback, but I was a likely starter now on defense and would get many snaps it looked like at running back as well. I wasn't the little brother to Randy anymore.

Although we weren't best friends in elementary school, we were friends. The three-year period apart during grades 7-9 while he was at Lowes Grove and I was at Neal made us somewhat strangers when we reunited at Southern. Randy now spent all his free time with twins Ron and Don Gullie, his baseball buddies, and we rarely hung out. By our senior year, I began to wonder if Randy for some reason now resented me. Surely, I was not a threat to him in any way, but an incident during practice two weeks before our first game made me wonder how he felt about me now.

We were doing a live, full-contact scrimmage, and it certainly appeared that Randy set me up. Randy called the play in the huddle, a quick slant pass to me in my position as flanker. I would catch the ball and quickly turn up field if all went according to plan. Big Mac was in his position at middle linebacker, waiting to pounce on someone. When the ball was snapped to Randy, instead of throwing it immediately to me, he pump-faked three times, looking directly at me. This drew Mac's attention and alerted him to the play. Since the ball was not thrown immediately, I continued my 45-degree angle slant route, taking me directly into the path of Mac. When Randy finally threw the ball, it was in front of me, and I had to dive to catch the errant pass. While airborne, I crossed into the airspace of Mac, who hit me harder than I've ever been hit before. The contact sounded like a bomb had exploded, and a feeling of electricity surged through my body. I somehow held on to the ball but was now flat on my back on the ground, struggling to breathe. Everyone stopped, and the practice field grew silent. Was I paralyzed? Would I be able to get up? Would I be able to play ever again?

Coach Davis and Doc Blake stood over me. Coach spoke first, "Tony, you ok, Son? Can you move everything?"

"I … I … I think so, Coach," I said through labored breaths as I was started to wiggle my toes and then move my legs. "I'll be ok. Did I catch the ball?"

"Yeah boy, you caught the ball," Coach laughed, knowing now that I was alive, and there were no serious injuries. "Let Doc help you to the sidelines, and you take a few plays off."

As Doc Blake and one of the trainers helped me off the field, I looked over at Randy. He was on the defensive side of the ball, talking to Mac, and it looked like they both were laughing. Randy almost got me killed, and now he was laughing? Did he do this on purpose? I knew we were no longer very close, but had I gone from his friend to his enemy? The pain from Mac's vicious hit was nothing compared to the pain I felt from not knowing the answers to these questions.

The start of my senior season was only a few weeks away, and I wondered where I stood with the captain of our team.

# CHAPTER 13

## THE JOURNEY BEGINS

Finally. After all these years of waiting. After so much hard work. All the anticipation … all the hype … all the hopes and dreams of our families and our community … from Pop Warner to junior high and now to the BIG time. High School football. Senior year. First real game. Let's get it!

Our opponent was Orange High School, and in the lead-up to the game, their coach, Jay Gilbo, seemed to employ some psychological warfare. He used the old coaches' trick of laying it on extra thick in your adulation of your adversary. The day before facing our team on August 26th to kick off the season for both squads, he held nothing back in his praise for us. "They've got a lot of people returning. The word I get is that they have a good chance to win the state championship."[15]

As I sat on the bench in front of my locker in our field house, carefully packing my equipment for the short 30-minute trip to Hillsborough, I tried to stay confident. I had experienced success in Pop Warner and junior high. I had proven myself for two years on the jayvee team. This was so different, though. This was THE VARSITY! My familiar foe named fear slithered up beside my bench, crawled up my back, and wrapped itself around my neck, making it difficult to breathe.

I didn't join in the conversations, the friendly insults, or the innuendos questioning each other's manhood not because I was above that or better than anyone else; my total focus at that moment was on what would take place in a few hours on a rectangular plot of earth in Orange County. Coach Davis would wait until shortly before the game began to announce the starting lineups. Would I hear my name called, or would I begin the season as a backup?

Although Stacey had played well during the scrimmage against Durham High the week before and knew his assignments at outside linebacker as well as I, there was still a level of confidence that I felt about winning the starting spot there. After all, I took the majority of the reps with the first-team unit in the week leading up to this game, and it appeared that I had the inside track to take the field first when our defense lined up. As far as offense, two of our three running back positions were a lock. Darryl would be fullback and Stanley would be tailback, but the starter at the wingback position was not so clear. Would it be Antuane, David Young, or me? In a few hours, all my questions would be answered, but for now, it was time to make my way to our team bus, an older model that also doubled as the school activity bus and without doubt had seen its better days.

As I climbed the three steps to the top landing of the bus, I was hoping to find an empty seat, longing to gain control of the inner emotions that sought to overtake me. I usually sat with Adam, and since seventh grade, he had been like that favorite blanket that a young child has, always there to offer security. A great fear of every teenager is to enter the lunchroom or step on a bus and have no one to sit with … to feel alone. As long as Adam was there, I knew I had a friend. For all these years, I never had to worry about sitting by myself.

On this August afternoon, however, I needed to sit and talk with someone else. Someone that looking back, I didn't know too well. My inner dilemma desperately demanded that I have a deep discussion with one Tony Bazen. He needed encouragement. He needed to know that it didn't matter that he was not born in Durham. It didn't matter now what type of home he lived in. It didn't matter that he was wearing the only pair of jeans that he owned. It didn't matter about all the cold winter nights when there was no money for kerosene oil to heat their home, forcing the family to turn on the eyes of the stove, seeking warmth. It didn't matter that many of his teammates had cars already, but he was dependent upon a friend for rides. It didn't matter that he, as always, was the smallest guy on the team. All that mattered right now was that he, like all the other boys on the bus that day, had on a white jersey emblazoned with red numbers. There was a good chance, as unlikely as it would have seemed a few years ago, that Coach Davis would call out his name as a starter for the first game tonight. Tony Bazen needed to know that regardless of everything, he belonged.

Adam must have thought it strange when I bypassed him and found an empty seat near the back of the bus in front of team manager Tim Lassiter. I had known Tim since way back at Bethesda, and he had always been extremely large for his age. As the years passed by, I found that his heart was much bigger than his body, and it was made of pure gold. Everyone liked Tim, and his smile and thick country accent were the balms I needed for my troubled soul.

"Hey, Bazen. Why ya' sittin' all the way back here?" The back of the bus carried the trainers, managers, and the equipment, and Tim was shocked to see a player there. "I'm just here to keep an eye on you to make sure you're behaving," was all I could think to say. Tim was an avid UNC fan, and I was one of the few NCSU fans at Southern (Durham was Duke and UNC country), so we talked a little ACC basketball. The Wolfpack basketball team, led by Coach Valvano, had a miracle run to the national title earlier that year, and State fans like me were still basking in the glory of this. I had backed the Pack since 1974 when I watched a little NCSU point guard named Monte Towe help led them to their first national championship. Although high-flying forward David Thompson, who is considered one of the greatest NCAA basketball players of all time, and gargantuan seven-foot-four-inch center Tommy Burleson garnered most of the headlines, it was the diminutive five-foot-seven-inch Towe that captured my attention. A little guy playing a big man's game was someone with whom I could relate, and watching Towe experience success in the red and white of NC State began a lifelong love affair with the Wolfpack, leading me one day to pursue a degree there.

"You think they gonna be good again this year?" Tim asked. As I was about to impress him with my knowledge of State basketball prospects for the coming season, suddenly there was a thunderous voice that filled the cabin of the bus, emanating from a small body. The Tasmanian Devil had issued his decree. "I don't want to hear another sound until we get to Orange High School. All of you sit quietly. Get your mind on the game!"

Orders delivered, Coach Davis sat down, the bus engine started, and we began our trek to Hillsborough. No one dared defy the edict that had been passed down. For the next 30 minutes, all I heard was the roar of the bus engine and some occasional muffled words coming from the front of the bus, where the coaches were still busily preparing our strategy for the evening.

I only had half an hour to try to convince the person in the seat with me that although he was small, this moment was not too big for him.

# CHAPTER 14

## SO FINE

Old Faithful, our trusty team bus, lumbered down I-70W for about 10 minutes and then merged onto I-85S towards the big city of Hillsborough, population 6,087 as of the 2010 census. I was looking out the window from the back of the bus, but I was oblivious to all the greenery that flashed by my eyes as we traveled down this thickly tree-lined interstate. Coach Davis had told us to get our minds on the game, and I was 100% obedient, not able to think about anything else. I was so focused that for the first time in weeks, I went an entire waking hour without thinking about Karen. She promised to find a way to be there for the season opener, but my mind was not on a girl but on a game.

I was jolted out of my trance by the backend of the bus bouncing roughly over a speed bump that was in the Orange High School parking lot. The Spartans had arrived, and in a flash, we were all out of our chariot and into the locker room, preparing to enter the enemy's lair. Orange's mascot was the Panthers, but hopefully, this would not be some "Christians thrown to lions" type outcome in the colosseum that night.

I took off my white Spartans' jersey with the red 47 on it, removed my blue jeans, and began the process of donning my armor for the battle that would shortly take place. Spartans' gray cut-off undershirt to wear under my shoulder pads -Check! Jockstrap -Check! Girdle containing hip pads and butt pad. Check! Red football pants with thigh pads and knee pads. Check! Long, thick white socks with red stripes near the top. Check! White cleats. Check! Shoulder pads. Check! White jersey over shoulder pads. Check! White wristbands for each arm. Check. Helmet. Check!

I stood in the visitor's locker room with armor on, helmet in hand, awaiting my marching orders. Coach Davis started reading off all the different starters for all the different groups. He began with special teams. Amazingly, he called out my name to start on the Kickoff Team. My name was called also for the Kickoff Return team. I was even selected to be a part of the Extra Point team. I was psyched up, and my excitement only grew stronger when I discovered I would be the starter at Will linebacker for our defense. The last group of starters to be announced was the Offense. The backfield starters would be Randy at quarterback, Darryl at fullback, Stanley at tailback, and…. Antuane at wingback. My heart sunk a little as by now I was greedy to be on the field the whole time.

We lined up in rows of four and walked towards the field. As we neared the field, we spied the gigantic banner that the cheerleading squad had designed that simply said, "GO SPARTANS -BEAT THE PANTHERS!!!" As they held the ends up of this massive paper sign, the SHS band blared what became our theme song that year, *Eye of the Tiger*. In 1982, Sylvester Stallone had unveiled another episode in his blockbuster movie series about an underdog boxer named Rocky who became world champ. For obvious reasons, I was inspired by this series, and *Rocky III* was my favorite. It had a great cast, a thrilling story, and the incredible theme song by the group Survivor. As *Eye of the Tiger* roared its tune throughout the stadium, the large contingent of SHS fans that had also made the trip down I-85 stood to their feet as we broke through the banner, ran to a spot near the visitor's sideline, formed a circle, and Tommy Upchurch came to the middle. Tommy yelled at the top of his voice the chant that became our anthem, and we repeated in unison every line.

We are the Spartans! *We are the Spartans!*
Count every man! *Count every man!*
Here we come! *Here we come!*
Here we stand! *Here we stand!*
Do or die! *Do or die!*
Our battle cry! *Our battle cry!*
We will win! *We will win!*
They will die! *They will die!*
Kill! Kill! Kill! Kill!

We won the coin toss and elected to defer our option to the second half, allowing our defense to be tested first. I heard the coaches screaming, "Kickoff team! Kickoff team!" and the 11 young men who had been selected for this unit gathered around Coach Davis, who gave us a quick pep talk. "All right, boys. This is it! This is what we've been waiting for. Let's get a good start. Go out there, and smash 'em in the mouth! Get out there and hit someone! Show 'em what you're made of! Show these boys some Southern football!"

With that, we lined up, and I took my position on the right end of the line, with strict instructions to NEVER let the ball carrier get outside me. The ball was placed on the kicking tee on our own 40-yard line, and we put our feet on the 35, waiting for the whistle that would signal our long kicker Cheeseburger to start towards the ball. We would follow a half step behind him and by the time he kicked the ball, the five-yard buffer would act as a runway, propelling us like missiles downfield, ready to blow up anything that stood in our way.

It seemed like an eternity passed by as we waited for the whistle to blow. I looked downfield at the imposing 11-man army that stood before me, clad in black pants and jerseys and wearing bright orange helmets. They looked huge and hungry, ready to devour all 139 pounds of me. I began to doubt myself again. Was I ready for the varsity? Could I compete at this level? As my body tensed, my mind raced, and my heart beat audibly, the official blew his whistle loudly and threw down his right arm, signaling the battle had begun. Eleven Spartans clad in white jerseys and red pants raced down the field to do battle, seeking to slay 11 black-clad Panthers. My senior season had finally begun!

The ball traveled end over end, straight down the middle of the field, and landed in the arms of a Panther on his own 10-yard line. The Panthers all began to move to their right, our left, attempting to form a wedge to open a hole for the ball carrier. I stayed in my lane on the right side of the field, like I had been taught, and then angled toward the ball as their swift running back attempted to find a lane. Stacey broke through the wall of black jerseys and felled the ball carrier, hitting him with a loud thud. We all ran towards him, slapping him on the back and shoulder pads, yelling encouragement. There was some pushing and shoving and a lot of trash talk. The men in black were fired up for us, and for some reason thought they could intimidate us with their words. No way. This extracurricular activity after the first play was a preview of what would take place the entire game, as the Panthers played dirty from start to finish, even roughing our punter three different times.

"Good hit, Stacey!" I screamed to my friend as he ran off the field. The first play was over, and although I encountered no enemy fire from my side of the field, I had survived.

Our defense huddled around defensive captain Mac McClure as he relayed the instructions from Coach Shankle, our defensive coordinator. "4-4, 4-4!" Mac repeated, signaling that we would begin with our base defense of 4 down linemen and 4 linebackers. I stood behind our massive line as the play call was given, realizing afresh how big and strong our front four were, with Mike and Cheeseburger at the tackles and Charles Lee and Antuane at the ends. I stood beside Kevin as we huddled together, and he seemed even more massive tonight. Kevin and Big Mac were manning the middle at inside linebackers, and Tommy and I lined up on the outside. In the secondary as our last line of defense, we started Stanley and Jay at the corners and Brent at safety.

Tommy was Sam (strongside) linebacker, and I was Will (weak side) backer. The strong side is usually the side of the ball where the most offensive players line up or the wide side of the field, where more plays are typically run since there is more room to operate. Coach Davis decided to use a variation of this, having Tommy on the strong side when there was an extra lineman on one side, and since I was faster than Tommy, I always lined up on the wide side of the field. "4-4, 4-4! Ready ... Break!" As Mac screamed "Break," we said it in unison with him, and all clapped our hands at the same time, then made our way to our positions on the field.

The ball was on the left hash mark, so I lined up on the right side of the field. The Panthers broke their huddle and approached the line of scrimmage. "Twins right, twins right!" I screamed out, alerting our defense that there were two receivers on my side, and I shifted two yards to my right since I had pass coverage responsibility in the flats, an area from about one to five yards off the line of scrimmage. The Panthers' quarterback barked out the signals, and the ball was snapped. I took a 45-degree step to my right since my first responsibility was to defend against the pass and then saw the QB hand the ball to their big, burly fullback on a dive play up the middle. I planted my right foot firmly in the freshly cut turf and exploded towards the action. The ball carrier was engulfed in a sea of red, hit first by Mike and then by Mac, and then swallowed up by a host of other red-clad warriors after only a one-yard gain.

Second and nine. We huddled again. Mac got the defensive signal from Coach Shankle and relayed it to us. "4-4, Will Fire. 4-4, Will Fire. Ready ... Break." As we clapped our hands together and left the huddle for our respective positions, I was so pumped up! The coach had called for me to blitz on this play, meaning that as soon as the ball was snapped, I would immediately vacate my normal two x two pre-snap position (two yards outside of our defensive end and two yards off the line of scrimmage) and immediately charge into the opposition backfield to try to disrupt the play.

The Panthers came to the line, sending one wide receiver to the right. I called out, "Basic, Basic," and took my position, being careful not to show my intentions of blitzing at the snap of the ball. "Hut 1, Hut 2," and out of the corner of my eye I saw the ball move, and like a drag racer who saw the green light flash, I burnt rubber off my cleats heading for the Orange backfield to wreak all the havoc I could. The quarterback tossed the ball to the tailback on a sweep to my side with the fullback leading the way. I crashed down hard, avoiding the wide receiver who was attempting a crackback block on me, and it was now two on one, as I stared at the oncoming fullback and the running back who was using him as a human shield. It was Oklahoma Drill all over again and just like the time years before when I was a ten-year-old for the Bethesda Cowboys, I met the blocker with all the force I could muster, sending him careening to my left and leaving the RB in my sights. The violent collision with the fullback left me off-balance, and the ball carrier faked inside, then sped up and went outside, attempting to get around the corner. Just when he seemed that he would get around me for a big gain, I planted with my left foot and lunged diagonally to my right, my body fully stretched out parallel to the ground. I reached for his feet as I soared through the air and was able to grab his right foot and send him tumbling to the ground for a two-yard loss.

As I pulled myself off the turf, I was mobbed by teammates. I was met my Big Mike McClure, who slapped me hard upside the right side of my helmet and said, "Good stop, Boy!" Other teammates hit me on the shoulder pads and there were shouts like "They can't move the ball on us. It's gonna be a long night for the boys in orange!" As I made my way back to the huddle, I heard the PA announcer say, "Tony Bazen on the tackle for Southern," a proclamation to the world and most importantly to me that I belonged.

The Panthers tried to pass on third down, and Antuane brought the heat from his left end position, bringing the QB to the ground and forcing a punt. Orange's defense started every bit as stout as ours. Their normal alignment was a 5-2, with five down linemen, two linebackers, and four in the secondary. They went all out against us to stop the run and switched to a 6-2 alignment, stacking the line of scrimmage with six defenders, two linebackers, and only three on the backend, almost daring us to pass. Their strategy worked on our first two possessions, as their swarming defense bottled up Darryl. Each time they stopped our fantastic fullback, they taunted us.

"Get up, McGill! You ain't so bad! McClure, you can't block me! Is that all you got, Sowell? You boys are overrated! You're not that good."

They say it's better to let sleeping dogs lie, and their trash talk was the alarm we needed. On our third possession, now fully awake, we finally took to the air. With the Orange defense still crowding the line to stuff Darryl, Randy faked a handoff to him, drifted back to pass, and found Stanley speeding down the sideline, hitting him in stride for a 44-yard touchdown. Mike Wiggins kicked the extra point, giving us a 7-0 lead as the first quarter closed.

Our defense continued to dominate the entire first half, completely bottling up the Panthers and giving the ball back to our offense. Our big offensive line finally began to open holes for Darryl in the second quarter, and he rambled for 72 yards in this quarter alone, culminated by a three-yard touchdown run shortly before halftime. The extra point attempt was blocked, but we went into the visitor's locker room with a 13-0 lead. Coach Davis, however, was far from happy. "You're playing like a bunch of pansies out there. This team should not even be on the same field with you. Mike, Mac, Tommy, Duke, Arthur, Kevin, Todd … when are you going to block somebody? I'm tired of seeing black shirts in our backfield. Now let's get out there and kick their butts!"

Coach's words were heeded, and our offense was a machine in the second half, scoring almost at will. We opened the third quarter with the ball and went on a long, 11-play drive, culminated by a play that became a favorite goal-line play for us, I-Right, Option Right, in which Randy could either give the ball to the fullback, fake it to him and pitch it to the tailback, or fake it to the fullback and just run it in himself. Near the goal line all year, Randy always either handed the ball to Darryl or ran it in himself, not risking a backward pitch this close to pay dirt. He chose the second option here, capping off the long drive by faking the ball on a handoff to Darryl and then walking in the end zone untouched. Randy also ran in a two-point conversion, giving us a 21-0 lead, and the game was all but over then.

Realizing that they could not beat us on the scoreboard, the Panthers tried to turn the game into a WWE match, with late hits, dirty play, and continual jawing. The dam of emotions that had been building finally burst, and a brawl ensued, with Jay caught in the thick of it. Spanky, never one to back down from a fight, was right there to protect one of his brothers. When the officials finally separated everyone, Jay got ejected from the contest, but an important point was made in the initial game of the season. If you mess with one of the Spartans, you better be prepared to fight us all.

Early in the final quarter, Randy hit Mac McClure on a 43-yard touchdown pass, and after Allen Tilley blocked a punt and recovered it in the end zone, we led 36-0. Coach cleared the benches after this score, and my night was now done. Stacey went in for me on defense and played well, but the second-team defense allowed a late drive and score by Orange, so we lost our shutout. The final score was an impressive 36-8.

For the first game, things couldn't have gone much better for our team. We racked up 329 yards of total offense and five different people found the end zone, led by Darryl with 142 yards and a touchdown, and Randy, whose first game of the year was perhaps the best he would have all year, as he threw two touchdown passes and ran for another. As well as the offense played, however, it was the defense that deserved the game ball. Before the first-team defense was taken out, we had held the Panthers to 53 yards, only three first downs, and had kept them off the scoreboard. It was a dominating performance by our team, in particular, our defense.

After lining up at midfield and shaking hands with our opponent, we walked off the field towards the locker room. I walked alongside Jay, as it looked like my friend needed a little encouragement after being ejected from the game. He had a multitude of questions. Would the coaches be upset with him? Would this cost him his starting job? Would there be any repercussions after cursing, fighting, and getting thrown out of the first game of the season? Any fears he harbored were quickly squelched when we walked past Coach Dodson, who in his unique Southern drawl loudly said, "Ole Kapiko here tryna' be Bruce Lee out there tonight!" Everyone in earshot of us burst out laughing, and with that one sentence, Jay knew that all was forgiven.

On the way to the locker room, I passed by Karen, who looked particularly beautiful as she stood beside her parents, and she smiled brightly at me. She was a cheerleader but not very knowledgeable about sports; she just knew we had won the game and had heard my name called a few times. "You played good, Tony." I smiled sheepishly and could only think of this response. "I'm glad you came tonight. Hope to see you tomorrow. I'll call you."

I waved bye to her and, as I was entering the locker room, was greeted at the door by Tim, who had a clipboard in his hands. One of his gameday duties was to be our statistician and as I was about to pass by him, he put his hand into my chest and stopped me. "Guess what, Bazen? You led us in tackles tonight. Eight solos and two assists. Not a bad night."

We took off our armor, showered, changed into our street clothes, and boarded the bus. As we waited for Coach Davis to finish his interviews and join us for our chariot ride home, the Orange coach stepped up onto the bus to speak with our team. I don't remember why Coach Gilbo felt the need to invade our territory or exactly what he said, but Antuane, who was sitting near the front of the bus, had a bold question for him, "Coach, why does your team play so dirty?" The black-shirted coach was caught off guard by the question and was speechless for what seemed like an eternity. He was visibly angry now but wisely decided to deflect the question and simply say, "Good luck the rest of the season," and departed from the enemy's lair.

"Antuane, you're crazy, bro," Stacey shouted out from the back of the bus. "I can't believe you asked that man that."

Antuane, although just a junior on this senior-dominated team, was a natural leader, never afraid to speak his mind. "That man's responsible for his team, and they played like punks. You saw what they tried to do to Tony. Three roughing the punter penalties. Then they tried to gang up on Jay. That don't fly, man. Somebody needed to call him out on that."

It would be many years later before I had the confidence like Antuane to speak up and speak out, but I would have fought for any of my brothers on that team. Whether we played together for many years or just a few, we were a family, and family may have disagreements, but family has each other's backs. Jay said it well, "We all got along so well and had fun in the locker room, even with such a diverse group of guys." We didn't realize it fully then as our life experiences were too limited, but the guys on that team truly loved each other.

On the way home, I sat behind David Andrews, a tall and slender junior who was a superb athlete but was now buried on the depth chart behind seniors. His day in the sun would come, just not this season. David was handsome and cool as a cucumber, a guy with great hair who never had trouble getting a date. He had some earphones on and was singing an

R&B song from Howard Johnson that had become a hit the year before entitled *So Fine*. I could hear the words as they blared through his headphones:

> *So fine; So fine, blow my mind.*
> *Hold your head back,*
> *Now, close your eyes.*
> *Hey girls, tell me that you're fine.*
> *Hold your head back,*
> *Lean to the side.*
> *Hey fellas, ain't she fine?*
> *Baby baby baby,*
> *So fine.*
> *So fine, blow my mind.*

As I replayed the events of the last three hours, I could hardly believe all that had taken place. We had handily won our first game. I played most of the game and led the team in tackles. Karen was there with her whole family, and her smile seemed to show that her feelings for me were getting stronger by the day. The young man on the bus seat with me on the ride to the game had so many questions, and it seemed like now all of his questions had been answered.

As we drove now north on I-85 heading towards southern Durham, I held my head back on the seat of the bus, smiled into the darkness, and looked skyward. Everything seemed *So Fine*.

# CHAPTER 15

## WHEN THE GOING GETS TOUGH

When I woke up at the break of dawn on Saturday morning following my first varsity football game, I was sore but satisfied, exhausted but exhilarated, and despite catching a cramp in my left calf when I stretched out, I bounded out of bed as the cramp subsided and headed straight for our gravel driveway. The newspaperman delivered *The Durham Morning Herald* to our driveway like clockwork at 6:05 each morning, and I was so excited to see what morning sportswriter Charles Chandler would say about our opening game.

I described "Big Al" Carson earlier, and Chandler was the antithesis of Carson. Chandler was a tad younger, much slimmer, clean-cut, and had boyish good looks. Chandler dressed more smartly and neater in his polo shirts and Dockers pants. Even though Carson sometimes wore a tie, his wrinkled shirts and generally disheveled appearance were a sharp contrast to the "everything in place" Chandler. Carson was the prototypical Carolina Boy, born and bred in the state, and content to stay in small-town America. He worked for the evening paper until it was combined into one daily paper, *The Herald Sun,* giving a total of 32 years to covering sports in Durham. Chandler was far more ambitious, using his gig in Durham as a springboard to bigger and better things, landing a job with the prestigious Charlotte paper *The Charlotte Observer,* where he eventually went from covering high school football to becoming the beat writer for the Carolina Panthers.

I quickly made my way from my bedroom in the back of our double-wide to the front door, stepped off our wooden porch, and gingerly walked barefoot across the jagged rocks to retrieve the paper. As was my routine, I walked back inside, placed the newspaper on the kitchen table, slid off the rubber band that kept it securely rolled up, laid it out flat, and opened it to the only section that mattered to me: Section B. A picture on the front of the sports section immediately grabbed my attention. There I was on the front, and although the focus of the picture was on Kevin and his interception in the Orange game, it was so exciting to see my picture in the paper. Chandler wrote, "The win was an impressive beginning for what is supposed to be a banner season for the Spartans, who are favored to win the Triangle 3-A Conference."[16]

Things got even better the next morning when I opened the Sunday paper and looked again for Chandler's comments. The words he wrote on this Sunday were literally life-changing. "Monty Davis called Tony Bazen the best Will (weakside) linebacker he's ever had. That's pretty strong."[17] Did I just read this correctly? Did Coach truly think this about me? I was just concerned about being good enough to be a part of the team. Like other coaches I had before him, he saw something in me that I struggled to see in myself. Chandler said that Coach's words were "pretty strong." What an understatement! These were mountain-moving words ... life-giving words ... "I believe in you even if you don't believe in yourself" words.

Everything seemed to be coming up roses for my team and me. Next up on our schedule was a home game against Dunn High School. The Green Wave were two-time defending conference champs and had loudly celebrated after the previous year's 22-6 victory which knocked us out of the state playoffs. Mike McClure was still angry about last year's defeat. "There's going to be revenge. Last year they were laughing at us after the game. We've got a pep rally Friday. We're going to get all psyched up. This game means everything to us. Friday night I will put all out. It will probably be the hardest game I play all year."[18]

Mike's prediction was spot on as we played an almost flawless game, physically manhandling Dunn. In what was billed as the game of the year between the two favorites to win the Conference title, it was no contest. We dominated the Green Wave in every facet in a convincing 35-8 drubbing. Statistically, we outgained them 280 yards to only 120. Our defense was stout once again, holding Dunn to only 5 first downs.

We were up 28-8 at the half and didn't let up in the second half. Even after extending the lead to 35-8, Coach Davis left the first team in, and our defense did indeed exact some revenge after halftime, allowing only 30 yards total and no first downs. It was a total beatdown.

Even more scary for upcoming opponents was our dynamic running back duo of Darryl and Stanley. Darryl's bruising running between the tackles and Stanley's sprinter's speed that made him a threat to break a long run at any time made our offense virtually unstoppable. Both of them rushed for 120 yards against Dunn, and Darryl added three touchdowns as well. We had Thunder (Darryl) and Lightning (Stanley) in our backfield, and no team in the state looked capable of slowing us down.

Coach Davis was especially pleased with this win. "You don't like to get beat three years in a row. It really bothered me. They were really coming at us. They had nine men up front, and we just went straight at them, straight football- dives and belly-give-to-full. Kevin and Mac just knocked them off the football. The whole offensive line did a real good job. Anytime you have two backs with 120 yards each, you know the line is doing its job."[19]

Things just continued to get better on the Monday following the big game with Dunn when we achieved something that no other SHS team had ever accomplished. When the first Associated Press state rankings for 1983 were released, we were voted the #1 team in the state. Coach Davis tried to downplay the significance of the ranking. "If the Associated Press thinks so, fine, let them. I think it's kind of nice. Of course, it doesn't win you a title, but it does create some conversation. It's better to be there at the end of the season."[20]

I was playing for the #1 team in the state and was not just on the team, but a starter. We had the best team in school history and looked virtually unstoppable. Things were progressing well with Karen, and her dad, Paul, seemed to genuinely like me. He had even volunteered for our home games to be a part of the chain gang, the men who held the first down marker and the sticks joined by a 10-yard length of chain. Paul had two daughters, and it seemed like I was becoming the son he never had. My dad had never seen me play football and here was my girlfriend's dad holding the chains so he could watch from close up. Since Karen and I were now seeing each other on Saturdays and Sundays and I had no transportation of my own, Paul generously agreed to let me drive Karen's beautiful Midnight Blue '74 Camaro with Keystone rims home each Friday night. The Pizza Hut off Roxboro Road would fill with SHS students after every home game, and after a victory celebration there, I would drive Karen home in the Camaro. I kept it until Sunday afternoons when she would drive me home from dinner at her house. Life was good.

The saying is, however, that all good things must come to an end. For our team and me, the next few weeks proved this maxim to be true. Although we would win our next game, a home contest against South Johnston, we suffered a devastating loss after only four minutes had elapsed in the first quarter. After forcing the Trojans to kick on their first possession, Darryl and Stanley went back deep to receive the punt. Darryl stepped up to field the punt but mishandled it, and that's when a disaster struck that threatened to derail our dream season.

Coach Davis had a perfect vantage point of what happened, since it transpired near the home sidelines, just yards away from where he was standing with his arm around Randy's shoulder pads, preparing to give him the play to start our first drive of the game. "It was kind of a freak thing. There was a big scramble after the fumble by Darryl and Stan had barely gotten there. During the pileup, some player hit his knee."

Our team trainer, John Blake, revealed the severity of the injury to Stanley's right knee. "In the length of time I've been at Southern, it's the worst injury we've had. And it's the worst I've seen on the high school level. When I was at East Carolina, I saw several that were comparable." Stanley was taken to Durham County General Hospital that night and underwent emergency surgery, fitted with a full leg cast that he wore for six weeks, and then later a special brace that he wore an additional six weeks. It was such a tragic end to a great athletic career, and one of my lasting memories from my senior year is that of Stanley limping out on the court for the last home basketball game of his senior season and playing just a few minutes on Senior Night, but noticeably limping the whole time.

Stanley was more than a great athlete; he was a great human being. It was honestly not a big surprise that he became a pastor after graduation. Coach Davis echoed the sentiment felt by us all. "It's a great loss, not so much from the standpoint of the team athletically, but individually. Stan is a fine, fine young man. I know he will miss the game, too. He's quite a competitor. This hurts me so much for him. The team goes on whether I'm here or Stanley's here, but this is just very unfortunate for him."

In the heartbreak of the moment that September night, I saw a side of Coach that I had never seen before. After Stanley was carted off the field on a stretcher, loaded up into a waiting ambulance, and whisked away for surgery, there was an eerie silence that pervaded the capacity crowd. All of us were emotionally crushed as well, but the game had to go on.

Randy ran the play that Coach had given him, and I now stood beside our usually fiery, hard-nosed coach waiting to be given the next play to relay to Randy. Coach had his arm around my shoulders and with his headset on, was communicating with coaches in the press box area above, discussing the next play. As he prepared to give me the next play, his voice quivered, and for the first and only time in my life, I saw Monty Davis cry.

Stanley's loss made it tough for us to focus on the task at hand, and facing a team returning 18 starters from the year before, we became involved in the only close contest we would face during the entire regular season. Although we never trailed in the game, at halftime we held a razor-thin 7-6 lead and actually led only 15-14 with 8:26 to play after a 47-yard run by Trojan star running back Eric Morris. Displaying the heart of a champion, we went on a time-consuming drive to extend the lead to 22-14. A Trojan fumble after a sack and recovery by Mike McClure gave us the ball with three minutes to go, and Allen Tilley scored a late touchdown to make the final score 28-14.

With Stanley out of commission, we no longer had our Thunder and Lightning attack. We would need to lean heavily on Darryl from here on out, and he wouldn't disappoint. His 34 carry, 206-yard, two-touchdown performance became just another day at the office for him the rest of the year. "I knew deep down I had a load on my back," Darryl admitted. "I just did all I could. I played my heart out. It's a big loss for us."[21] Stanley's injury probably cleared the way for all the individual awards that Darryl would eventually win later that year, but the loss of our most versatile weapon cast a huge shadow over our state title aspirations. "We just have to go on," Coach said. "Naturally, you don't lose Stanley and not be limited somewhat in what you're going to do, but we're going to be ok. Somebody else will just have to pick up the slack."[22]

I was one of those called upon to pick up the slack. I replaced Stanley at starting running back on offense and also now was the deep man beside Darryl on kickoffs and punts. I was excited about the extra roles, but now would rarely come off the field at all. There would be games later in the season when I never left the field of play.

Week 4 was an away game against Oxford Webb, and "Big Al" again emphasized the impact of Stanley's loss. "Southern will surely miss Stanley Faison as he was their top deep threat in the passing game. Darryl McGill carried a big load last week, gaining 206 yards on 34 tries. Against Oxford, the Spartans will probably need more balance in the backfield, and they'll look to Tony Bazen, Antuane Simmons, and sophomore Alan Tilley." [23] Webb was a formidable opponent, and with the loss of Stanley, our margin for error was now super slim.

Doubt began to creep in now as to our ability to win it all. We slipped in the state rankings from #1 to #2, and some were wondering if our unbeaten streak would be stopped in Oxford against the Warriors. "The Spartans face their biggest test to date and maybe the biggest in the regular season. On the road, against a very physical and highly emotional team. It should be a dandy. Southern by 1."[24] Would Carson's prediction come to pass?

While everyone focused on Stanley's loss and the effect it would have on the offense, "Big Al" and others underestimated just how good our defense had already become. We completely shut down the Warriors, forcing eight turnovers (five fumbles and three interceptions), had seven sacks (three by Cheeseburger and two each from Mike and Antuane), and recorded our first shutout. The game was over for all intents and purposes in the first quarter when we took advantage of three Webb turnovers to score 21 points in less than 3 minutes on the way to a convincing 28-0 victory. Coach Davis loved hard hitting and was ecstatic about the thrashing we gave Webb. "That was a heck of a football team we played tonight. They had a lot of fumbles, but we were sticking them, baby. And when you're stuck like that, the ball's got to come out."[25]

I had a good game defensively, finishing with seven tackles, including two tackles for losses, and started at running back. Antuane, David,

Allen, and I filled two of the running back slots beside Darryl. Clint Williams also was called up from the jayvee to provide depth and scored on a 26-yard touchdown run. The five of us shuttled in plays to Randy, so I played about half of the snaps on offense. Although my main role was to block for Darryl, I even got a few carries.

A glorious night for our team took a negative turn towards the end of the third quarter. Darryl was tackled hard and remained writhing in pain on the ground, holding his right knee. Surely fate had not dealt us another cruel blow just a week after Stanley's injury. All the Southern faithful who had made the trip to Oxford held their collective breath, and all of us on the field took a knee and bowed our heads, whispering a prayer for Darryl to become like Lazarus and rise. Prayers answered, Darryl slowly rose to his feet and was helped to the sidelines by Doc Blake and our training staff, but he didn't return to the game.

Early in the fourth quarter, we called for a pass, and my responsibility on this particular play was to stay in the backfield and block for Randy, giving him time to find an open receiver. A huge Oxford lineman broke free up the middle, and I stepped to my left to block him. As I lowered my shoulder and planted both feet to absorb the impact from our collision, my back was twisted in an awkward position, and I felt intense pain when contact was made. When the play was over, I struggled to stand up straight without torrents of pain shooting up and down my back. I told no one and refused to leave the game. I had waited too long and worked too hard to become a starter; if I could walk, I would remain on the field. It was evident to me, however, as the final seconds ticked off the clock that after playing football for 10 years, I had my first significant injury.

Stanley out for the year. Darryl now a question mark. My back throbbing with pain. As we made the 40-minute trip back home, the mood on the bus was more that of a wounded team than a winning team. The adage says that "Adversity does not build character, it reveals it." We were now staring adversity squarely in the face, and our true character was about to be revealed.

# CHAPTER 16
## A WIN FOR THE CITY

I woke up on Saturday morning and didn't hop out of bed to go grab the newspaper, as was my custom. My back hurt even more than it had the day before. It was a chore to get up, and my big fear was missing time and losing my starting positions, especially on defense. Before getting the paper, I gingerly walked to the bathroom, being careful not to jar my back, and pulled open the mirror, behind which we kept some medicine. I grabbed the Tylenol bottle, struggled to open the childproof cap, and poured some tablets into my hand. Four came out, and I wasn't sure about the proper dosage for my condition, but this amount seemed like it might help. I never needed water or any liquid to swallow pills, so I gathered some saliva in my throat, and one by one quickly downed the pills.

After about an hour, my pain eased a little, allowing me to walk a little more normally. My weekend Saturday and Sunday dates with Karen were a highlight as normal, although my back discomfort annoyingly nagged at me the whole time. In the blink of an eye, it was Sunday night again. Time to drive back to my home with Karen in her Camaro, say goodbye, and then watch her drive away. I had girlfriends before, but she was different. It was not just that she was beautiful; it seemed like I could talk with her about anything. I was usually painfully shy but felt comfortable with her almost from the time we had met six weeks earlier. What was this feeling I felt deep inside? Was this love? If so, would I be so foolish as to give my heart to someone and risk it getting crushed?

My back was still hurting on Monday morning, so much so that I knew I needed to talk to Doc Blake. During the morning break, I made my way to his office and told him what I happened on Friday night and about the pain I had endured all weekend. There was a running joke amongst the team that Doc's remedy for every ailment was the same, "Put ice on it." True to form, Doc said that we needed to ice my back and start some treatments using electrical stimulation as soon as possible. I dressed for practice but could not participate, instead watching helplessly from the sidelines. It nearly killed me to watch Stacey fill my spot with the first-team defense as they went through some drills in preparation for our next game. After years of waiting and after climbing Everest, it seemed, would a back injury send me tumbling down to the bottom, never to return to the starting lineup again?

Our Week 5 opponent was Hillside High School, and this game carried added significance that extended far beyond the field. Although the two schools were less than 10 miles apart, they had never met in an official varsity football game. At one time more than 300 historically black high schools operated in North Carolina, but only five remained in 2021, with Hillside the oldest of the remaining quintet.[26] Hillside, remember, had been the high school for African Americans in Durham, and Southern for years was the Confederate flag-waving Rebels. Even 14 years after integration, White Flight from the city left Hillside still overwhelmingly black, and there was not even one white player on the Hornet's roster that year. This social significance was seemingly lost upon the players, as our only concern was keeping our undefeated streak alive.

Hillside was not known as a football power, although their 1943 team led by Coach Willie Bradshaw had finished unbeaten and unscored on. Were they the best team in the state that year? Sadly, that question will go forever unanswered as segregation erected a color barrier on whom they could play. Since the schools were integrated in '69, the Hornets' football fortunes had fallen on hard times, and the '83 Hillside team was no exception. They entered the game against us winless and were big underdogs. Hillside coach Sam Jones realized the opportunity this matchup presented for his Hornets. "I don't think they have any weaknesses. Their running game is just awesome. It's the best Southern team I've seen since I've been here. Our kids are excited about playing them for the first time. They're calling it the city championship."[27]

After watching practice from the sidelines on Monday through Wednesday, icing my back religiously each day, and getting the electrical treatments after practice, my back was still nowhere close to 100% but had recovered to the point that I wanted to attempt to practice on Thursday. On this day, we went through our entire game plan for Friday's contest and did a walkthrough of game situations. I knew if I didn't practice on Thursday, I might not play on Friday. The thoughts of not playing and forever losing my starting spot haunted me day and night that week.

Coach Bickel asked how I was feeling. "You good to go tomorrow?"

Without hesitation, I replied, "Yes Sir, I feel much better. I'm ready to play."

It was a definite lie, but one that seemed a matter of life and death at the time. I couldn't let this injury kill my dream season, so I exaggerated just a bit. Well, I exaggerated a lot because sudden movements were excruciating, and running was torture. I usually loved to smash ball carriers, but the thought of contact right now caused me to recoil. If the coaches allowed me to play after missing practice, would I help or hurt the team?

We were the Walking Wounded on Friday. Already without Stanley for the season, with Darryl nursing a sore knee, and now with my bad back, things got even dicier when Randy missed school on Wednesday with a virus and then left school early on Thursday with a high fever. Randy wasn't able to start the game, leaving backup Brent Ferrell to begin behind center.

I had dumped a handful of Tylenol into a napkin that morning, folded it up, and placed it in my bookbag before leaving for school. I figured I might need to take a couple before the game to knock back the pain. Two hours before kickoff, however, my back had significantly stiffened up to the point that all movement was labored. I felt conflicted, hurting too much to play but feeling like not playing might hurt me too much, as I could lose my starting

positions for good. In a last-ditch act of desperation, I reached inside my book bag, furiously dug around, and finally found the napkin with the Tylenol inside. I opened it up and counted eight pills, tilted the napkin towards my left hand, and let the tablets roll down. Were eight pills too many? Could a person overdose from this amount? I didn't think so but wasn't sure. My only real concern at the moment was for this pain to subside long enough for me to make it through this game, so I downed all of them.

Missing our starting quarterback and with Darryl at far less than full speed, it's no wonder that we struggled to move the ball. To make matters worse, Kevin went down with a knee injury in the first half, making things even more challenging. We jumped out to an early 12-0 lead, and it looked like the rout was on, but when Hillside star running back Brad Sullivan, who later played at UNC, scored shortly before halftime, we went to our field house clinging to a precarious 12-6 lead.

I don't think any of us remember much of what Coach Davis said at halftime, as our ears were tuned in to the smooth sounds that sifted through the cinderblock walls of our field house. We had heard about the award-winning, nationally renowned Hillside Marching Band, and we were hoping to be released early from the halftime pep talk, so we could watch the rhythmic, high-stepping Hornets do their thing. Their performances were legendary, but unfortunately, they were already exiting the field when we reappeared from our field house.

With our offense out of synch, the defense rose to the occasion in the second half, limiting Hillside to only 30 total yards after halftime. Mike McClure and Cheeseburger were beasts in the middle, dominating the line of scrimmage and totaling eight solo tackles each. This was one of my worst games, as I was in on just a few tackles, but I was just happy that I was able to play. I think we all felt a sense of relief when the game ended and were glad that, even though we had not dominated the game like most thought we would, our perfect record was still intact.

With all the setbacks that we faced, Coach Davis knew that we dodged a bullet. "I was very proud of our football team. We've met adversity and overcome it. We had Randy sick and Kevin sidelined, and we were constantly getting flagged for holding. I'm sure that this was not as pretty as some wins we've had, but it was a win where we had some adversity we haven't had before."[28]

We won the game, but in some ways, the real winner was the city of Durham. Although it took 14 years, the two schools in Durham perhaps most representative of the racial divide that existed for so many long years had met on the same field. Not a battlefield, but a football field. Not a Civil War but a battle for bragging rights in the city. No guns or weapons but just good, clean, hard-hitting football. And when the final buzzer sounded, ending the contest, both teams lined up and shook hands. We left the field with the most points; Hillside left the field with our respect.

# CHAPTER 17

## BREAKING FAMILY CURSES

After the game ended, we took off our equipment, placed it in our lockers, quickly showered, and got dressed. Adam, Stacey, and I got in his Volkswagen and headed to Pizza Hut. All the Southern players and cheerleaders usually made their way there after home games, and it was the place to be in Durham after 10:00 on Fall Friday game nights. The service was usually slow by this time of the night, but the pizza was delicious and somehow there was always beer available for underage high school students who desired it.

Karen could not go that night, so it was Boy's Night for me, and it was good to hang out with the guys. When you are in that moment, you don't realize how precious these times are. You don't fully comprehend that in less than a year all of this will be gone, as you and your classmates will scatter literally all over the earth after graduation. Maybe if we realized this, we would have treasured these moments in time more, or perhaps the realization would have been depressing, causing us to live in constant dread of the ticking clock that was slowly but surely stealing away our youth.

That night was a good night since alone with the boys, I also was able to drink some beer. It had been less than a year before when I had my first drink. Adam, Stacey, and I, since we stayed on jayvee as juniors, played our game that week on Thursday night. The varsity had a home game, so we put on our Spartans jerseys to identify us as football players and set off for the game. An older friend or relative of someone, I cannot remember who, bought us a couple of six-packs of Milwaukee's Best, a broke boy's Budweiser, and we sped past Southern High and turned left on the next street. We drove down about a mile, and Adam pulled the car over on the side of the country road. I'll never forget Adam taking out the contents of that brown bag and passing a beer to Stacey and me. They were seated up front; I was in the back, and when Adam turned and handed the 12-ounce beer to me, I was faced with a definite dilemma.

Because of what alcohol had done to my family, I had promised myself that I would never drink even one drop. I hated beer, wine, liquor … all of it. Or so I thought. I never imagined that one evening as a high school junior, I would be in the back of a Volkswagen, sipping on a beer. Thinking back, it is clear that my "hatred" of alcohol was nowhere near as strong as my love for acceptance. I wanted to fit in, and if that meant enduring the worst-tasting liquid that had ever entered my mouth, so be it.

The fact that Stacey became a good friend in high school is in reality no surprise. Our friendship was based on far more than the fact that we played the same position on the football field. We were friends because he was a good person, and there was mutual respect. Sometimes over the years when questioning someone about their attitude towards race, they would answer, "I'm not racist; I have a lot of black friends." Stacey was not my *black friend*. He was just my friend. At the time it may have been difficult, but I look back with gratitude at being a minority at East End Elementary in kindergarten. That year-long experience of being different and of learning to look past the amount of melanin in people's skin served me well throughout life.

One of my first black classmates at Bethesda was in a Grade 4/5 combination class. The only non-white student in Ms. Grantham's mixed-age class that year was a fifth grader named Redd, and he and I became fast friends. I remember him being so tall, but my memory could be jaded by my lack of size. He was indeed so much taller than me, partly because I was in Grade 4, he was in Grade 5, and partly because I was just SO small. I may have been his best and only friend that year. I distinctly remember Redd and me hanging out after school one day, and he pulled a fire alarm. When I was brought in for questioning, I didn't want to rat on Redd, so Ms. Grantham took us out in the hallway and gave both of us a good paddling. I took the punishment because Redd was not my black friend; he was my friend.

I remember an African American student named Reggie Grimes when I was in Grade 7 at Neal. He was the only black student in many of my GT (Gifted and Talented) classes, and I felt naturally drawn to him. We played football and basketball and got into much mischief together. Reggie was not my black friend; he was my friend. In junior high Adam became my best friend, but I had many people who were my friends whose skin was much darker than my own. They were not my black friends; they were my friends who just happened to be black.

It was very late when we left Pizza Hut, and as we cruised on I-70N, I was now in the front seat with Adam, and Stacey was in the back. For some reason that still escapes me to this day, I had a very foolish idea. Maybe it was the eight Tylenol, perhaps it was the beer, or maybe a combination of the two, but I rolled down the window on the passenger side door and decided I wanted to hang out of the car. Adam and Stacey laughed as we drove down the interstate and I had my body half in, half out of the car. And then my decision-making went from bad to worse. I told Adam to roll down his window as well, and I climbed completely out of my window and flung myself across the top of that Orange VW Bug, able with my left hand to grasp the other side of the car above the driver's side door window. With my body now sprawled across the Volkswagen with my left hand grasping the driver's side window door frame and my right hand the passenger's side door window frame, I pulled my body completely on top of the Bug, so that I was body surfing down I-70N. Poor decision-making at its finest, for sure.

After about a mile, Adam slowed down and pulled over to the shoulder of the road, and I climbed off the roof and slid back through the window into the car. At first, Adam was angry, wondering what in the world I was thinking, but then the three of us had a good laugh. It was approaching midnight, and I asked Stacey if he just wanted to spend the night at my house. He thought it would be ok, and Adam took us there, dropped us off, and drove away. Surprisingly, no one was home, as mom worked later than normal, and Brenda spent the night with a friend.

Perhaps the medicine was finally wearing off or my adventure on the top of the Bug reaggravated my injury, but whatever the cause, my back was now hurting again. I let Stacey use my single bed in my room at the back of our double-wide, and I slept on the couch. I was so tired and perhaps feeling the effects of my Tylenol cocktail of a few hours earlier and didn't hear my mom come home. I woke up around 8:00, went to my room, and awakened Stacey, and we both went to the kitchen to get some breakfast. Wanting to be a good host but possessing zero cooking skills, I decided that Stacey could have for breakfast what I normally did: Captain Crunch cereal. I told Stacey to sit in the dining room while I grabbed two bowls, a gallon of milk, and a big box of cereal.

The dining room was beside my mom's bedroom, and as Stacey and I talked and ate our breakfast, my mom was awakened and walked into the kitchen. Her eyes grew as large as saucers when she stepped into the kitchen and saw Stacey. "Good morning, Tony. Who's your friend?" Mom asked politely.

"It's my good friend, Stacey. He's on the football team. We went to eat pizza with Adam and the rest of the team after the game and were out late. Since it was almost midnight when we were leaving the pizza place, I just asked Stacey if he wanted to spend the night. His mom is on the way to get him now."

"It's very nice to meet you, Stacey. Did you have enough to eat? I can make y'all some eggs if you want."

"Nice to meet you, too, Mrs. Bazen. Tony's my boy. We've been good friends for several years now. The cereal was more than enough. I'm full now, but thanks for offering. And thanks for letting me stay last night."

Stacey's mom arrived a short time later, and he left. Momma was quiet, and as she washed dishes and tidied up the kitchen, I saw her do something unusual. To my amazement, she took the bowl and spoon that Stacey had used to eat his breakfast and threw them in the trash can. I love my mom and have rarely raised my voice to her, but this made me angry. "What are you doing, Momma? Why did you throw these away?" I asked as I fished them out from the garbage.

"Son," mom said in her usual calm, kind voice. "Why did you let a black boy stay in our home?"

"Momma, Stacey's one of my best friends. His color doesn't matter. I can't believe you threw those dishes away."

"We can't keep them. A black boy used them."

I put the bowl and spoon in the sink. "Momma, have you ever thought about all the times you eat out and how many different people have used those plates, forks, and spoons? And you don't even know how well they were washed. There's nothing wrong with this bowl and spoon. And there's nothing wrong with my friend."

In my mom's defense, I don't know of a kinder, gentler person than Rachel Bazen. If she stumbled across a person in need, no matter what their skin color, she would help if it were in her power to do so. Was she racist? Yes and no. The Oxford English Dictionary defines racism as "prejudiced against or antagonistic toward a person or people on the basis of their membership in a particular racial or ethnic group, typically one that is a minority or marginalized."[29] My mother was brought up with some prejudices against people of color to be sure, but she would be the last to be antagonistic towards anyone. She never harbored ill will or wished bad to happen to others. She was just brought up in a different era, with a different set of rules, and with different teachings. And she was taught wrong. Those deeply ingrained ideas, traditions, and mindsets are not uprooted quickly or easily. Growing up in the segregated South in a rural North Carolina town surrounded by fields that a generation earlier were worked by slave labor, she was like many in southern America who faced a steep learning curve when it came to race relations in the New South.

My father's upbringing in South Carolina was much the same; only some in his family fit the full definition of racism, as they were both prejudiced and antagonistic towards minorities. I didn't realize the full extent of this until after my father's untimely death in 2008. I was tasked with helping hastily prepare his funeral service, so I called my dear friend Tommy Steele, an African American pastor from Concord, NC, and asked if he would be willing to make the three-hour trip to Pamlico, SC to speak at my dad's memorial service. He graciously agreed to help me during this emotional rollercoaster of a time in my life, and I am forever grateful for this.

As Pastor Steele began to speak, I noticed that my dad's sister, brother-in-law, and several of my cousins that I hadn't seen for years stood up and walked out. I was bothered by this because it was rude, but just assumed they wanted to avoid hearing from a preacher. The real problem was not that they didn't want to listen to a preacher; they refused to sit and listen to a black preacher. When I stepped outside the funeral home, I was met by my aunt, uncle, and cousins who dropped a litany of F-bombs on me and cursed me as I have never been cursed before, all because I invited my pastor friend who happened to be black to speak at my father's service. I saw the ugly face of racism that day and experienced the venom that it can produce.

Family curses. Racism. Alcohol. I conquered the former, but the latter was an enemy I had yet to vanquish.

# CHAPTER 18

## A CONVERSATION WITH BIG AL

Excitement was building at school and around our community as we were now 5-0, halfway home to an undefeated regular season. When the AP rankings were released on Monday, we were again the top-ranked 3A team in the state. There was no time to celebrate or rest on our laurels as we had another enormous obstacle before us in the East Wake Warriors, who had beaten us four years in a row.

In what was billed the game of the week for the state, with no less than six major college prospects on the field and college recruiters littering the bleachers, we faced a team with more offensive firepower than perhaps any team we faced that year. The most lethal weapon in the Warrior arsenal was wide receiver Randy Marriott, who went on to have a productive college career at the University of North Carolina and even played in the Canadian Football League. Marriott was an incredible athlete, possessing 4.4 speed in the 40-yard dash, able to triple jump 48 feet, and having a vertical leap of 36 inches. In their first five games, he had caught 26 passes for 421 yards and scored eight touchdowns. East Wake coach Johnny Sasser repeated what was on the mind of all area coaches. "I had a coach tell me recently that he'd never seen a wide receiver capable of dominating a football game like Randy is."[30] With Darryl considered the state's top running back and Marriott the state's best receiver, offensive fireworks seemed to be guaranteed.

While we relaxed and recovered each weekend, our coaches were busy preparing the game plan for the week to come. When they unveiled our strategy on Monday for the big game on Friday, I immediately developed an enormous lump in my throat. The coaches decided I would follow Marriott the entire game, often tasked with man-to-man coverage on him. While I appreciated their confidence in me, I didn't know if I was up to the task. It didn't take long for me to find out.

On the Warrior's first play from scrimmage, Marriott split out wide to his right, and I followed him, lining head up on him at the line of scrimmage. Our coaches had watched the tape and knew that the Warriors loved to run a quick screen pass, with Marriott taking a quick jab step forward and then taking two steps back to catch a quick pass from his quarterback. Once he caught the ball with a little open space, he was almost impossible to track down. I knew that I had coverage help from our cornerback and even the safety would shift to Marriott's side of the field, allowing me to play him very tight on the line of scrimmage. When the ball was snapped, I recognized the play and reacted quickly, exploding toward Marriott when he took the two steps back to catch the quick pass. I collided violently with him just as the ball arrived, knocking him on his back and dislodging the ball from his hands. I was usually pretty quiet, but not after this play. Standing over Marriott as he lay on the ground, I looked directly into his eyes and screamed out, "It's going to be a long night, Marriott!" And it was a long night for Marriott and East Wake, as we pounded them 26-6.

After shaking hands with the vanquished Warriors, we gathered around Coach on the sidelines. He had been more fired up for this game than any I can recall. The East Wake coach had started coaching there around the same time as Coach Davis came to Southern, and they had somewhat of a personal rivalry as now the two veteran coaches in the Triangle 3-A. "Boys, I can't tell you how proud I am of you," our beloved coach said, his voice beginning to crack ever so slightly. "It's been four long years since we've beaten them. When they scored to start the third quarter, we could have choked, but you showed the world what you're made of.

That drive in the fourth quarter to put the game away was special. That was Big Boy Ball right there. We're not where we want to be yet, but we are on our way. 6-0 boys! We whipped dem Warriors! Now get in here!" With that, we gathered around Coach in a delirious mass huddle and started jumping up and down, chanting, screaming, and just enjoying the moment.

I wanted to get showered and dressed as soon as possible, so that we could join the pack at Pizza Hut. On this night, however, there was a welcome interruption. "Hey Tony," Coach Bickel yelled into the shower area, "Someone from the newspaper wants to talk with you." I still had soapsuds all over my body, but I rinsed off as quickly as possible and dried off hurriedly, excited about my first-ever interview. With only a towel covering the lower part of my body, I came out of the shower area and saw Charles Chandler waiting near my locker, notebook in hand.

Chandler didn't wait for me to dress, as he had a deadline to meet to get his article in, so I had my first interview with nothing covering my skinny frame but a towel. Wasting no time, he introduced himself and asked me a few questions. "Randy Marriott is one of the top receivers in the state. I understand that you were assigned to guard him tonight, and he had his lowest receiving total of the season. He only had three catches for 46 yards. How did you slow him down?"

I tried to speak with confidence. "I had heard a lot about him and had just seen him on TV last night. I tried not to let it worry me. I just wanted to do my job. The coaches had us well-prepared for the game, and I think we shut him off pretty good."[31] My first interview lasted less than two minutes, as Chandler saw Coach Davis now in our large coaches' office enveloped by reporters, and the young reporter didn't want to miss any quotes from the leader of the state's top-ranked team. He thanked me and hustled off, leaving me time now to get dressed and prepare for party time at Pizza Hut.

Coach Davis was beside himself as he talked to the mob of sportswriters that surrounded him. He was asked to comment on Darryl's effort, as our fantastic fullback had a whopping 239 yards on 33 carries to raise her per game average to almost 160 yards. "I don't know if I've ever seen a back run better than Darryl tonight. He just gave us super effort. Second and third effort."

Reporters then asked Coach about the defensive effort, holding the prolific East Wake offense to only one score. The Warriors entered the game averaging nearly 400 yards but were limited to 166 by the swarming Spartans. "I'm so proud of our defense. I thought we had a great defensive plan, and the kids executed it. We had to stop Marriott and then stop their quarterback. We didn't stop them every time, but you don't expect to completely stop talented and skilled athletes. We knew we couldn't play Marriott one on one, and Bazen did a great job covering him. Tony has been steady, steady, steady all season, and he's come up with the big play for us."[32] Before the reporters departed, Coach said, "You just have to give Bazen credit. The young man is superb. He's a little fellow, but somehow he always comes up with the big plays."[33]

Warrior's coach Sasser was thoroughly impressed with the Spartans. "Monty did a good job of preparing his kids. I know this win means a lot to them. They executed well on offense and played well on defense. It's hard to stop them off tackle, the way they block. That Mr. McGill, he's tough. He's very durable and a punishing type runner. They're just better than we are."[34]

Following my typical Saturday routine, I was up early in the morning and retrieved the paper, eager to read about our conquest the night before. Reading Chandler's article sent a chill up my spine. It was still surreal to see my name in the paper. "The team's sixth win, a 26-6 victory over East Wake Friday, was an impressive one. As has been the case for most of the season, fullback Darryl McGill and the Spartans' star-studded line were standouts. Against East Wake, however, a little man also played a key role. Tony Bazen, a 5-foot-10, 139-pound senior linebacker, led the team in tackles with eight solos and two assists. He also made sure wide receiver Randy Marriott, one of the state's top college prospects, was not a factor in the game."[35]

If I had a "do-over" with the brief interview with Chandler, I would have focused more on the outstanding job our defensive backs did against Marriott. I was primarily responsible for covering him on short routes, but Brent, Jay, and David Young had the far more difficult task of covering the speedy receiver when he went deep. They were more than up to the task and should have received more credit for shutting Marriott down. Before the year started, Coach Davis had concerns about our secondary, as Brent was the only returner there with any varsity experience. After the East Wake game, it was clear that the backend of our defense was up to any challenge thrown its way.

On Sunday, I opened the newspaper and found yet another surprise, as I had even been included as part of *The Week's Best,* highlighting area football players who stood out on Friday. I think I floated through the whole weekend, and things got even better after practice on Tuesday. Towards the end of practice, I saw Al Carson walk onto our practice field. This was not that unusual, as reporters often showed up to talk to Coach Davis or one of our stars. As we finished practice and started off the field, it shocked me when "Big Al" made a beeline for me and said, "Hey Tony, you had a great game against East Wake. I'd like to talk to you if you have time."

"Hello, Mr. Carson. I have some time. I'd be glad to talk to you."

The interview that day was a lengthy one compared to my first, but still somewhat a blur. I can't remember all that he asked or much of what I said. When practice ended the next day and Adam's VW pulled into my driveway, I didn't let the car come to a complete stop before I flung open the door and jumped out of the car. "Big Al" said that the article would be in the paper that day, so I was dying to find out what he said and what I said.

Carson began the article like this. "Where there's a will, there's a way. Tony Bazen is a 'Will' linebacker for the Southern Spartans and he's got the will to win. It's amazing that Bazen can start for a high school football team since he's only 5-foot-10 and 139-pounds (dripping wet). It's even more astonishing that he's a major cog in the defense for the number one team in the state."

The article talked about the unique friendship that Stacey and I shared. Even though we competed for playing time at the same position, we were close and sincerely wanted each other to succeed. Against East Wake, Coach decided to go with a Double-Will linebacker alignment to try to combat the Warrior's speed. This allowed Stacey and me to both play at the same time. They asked me about my relationship with Stacey, friends competing for the same position, and friends who were different colors. "We're real good friends. We've got a friendly competition. We like to see each other do well. When one of us is playing, the other is encouraging him."

Carson also interviewed Coach Davis for the article. His words meant more to me than he could ever realize. "Tony's a very intelligent player. He's academically strong. He understands the defenses and knows his responsibilities. He stays in the proper alignment. That helps him because with his size, he cannot afford to make a mistake. On offense, he's one of our better blockers. He has good hands. He returns kickoffs. He doesn't have a lot of speed or weight, but he has a lot of talent."

"Big Al" asked me if I ever imagined myself being a key member of the #1 team in the state. My response was completely honest. "I'm just happy to be playing right now. I had my doubts about whether I could play high school football or not. But I grew a lot last year. A lot for me, anyway." He also asked me about my lack of size and whether it was tough running the ball at 220-pound linemen or trying to tackle 190-pound backs. "My size doesn't bother me. When I've got the pads on, I'm just as big as they are. Really, it doesn't seem that hard."

The next day at school, our Principal Sam Keel called me to his office. "Tony, I read the article yesterday, and I want you to know how proud we are of you. You've had a great season, and I've never seen someone your size impact games so much. You are also getting things done in the classroom. Keep up the good work."

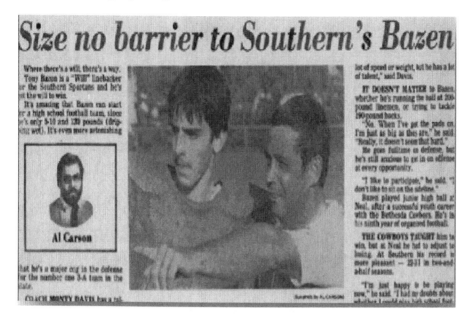

# Size no barrier to Southern's Bazen

**Al Carson**

COACH MONTY DAVIS has a vel.

"Yes Sir, Mr. Keel. Thank you." As I walked out of his office, it seemed like so much flashed before my eyes. It seemed like a wall of tears was forming at the back of my eyelids, waiting to be released like an unstoppable torrent. I quickly made my way to the restroom, found a stall, and closed the door. In the solitude of that moment, I wept. For years, I was tormented by this inner voice that continually screamed taunts of "You don't belong…you don't fit in…you're not big enough or good enough…you're an outsider." I had so often felt alone and inadequate and that I didn't measure up. I had almost killed myself to make good grades, spending hours each night on homework and preparing for tests and quizzes. I wanted to validate myself as someone who mattered…someone who had value. In athletics, my size meant I had to work twice as hard to keep up. I wasn't born with superior athletic ability; I had to continually work at it.

I remembered the literally thousands of hours through the years with a football in my hand, just tossing it in the air back and forth. I recalled all the times I played football against myself in our yard. I mentally rehearsed the one-on-one football games with Timmy Brewer, the only other friend before Stacey that ever spent the night with me. Timmy's dad also drank, and he understood my situation. I felt no judgment with him, and we both loved football.

My mind flashed back through the Bethesda years, being forced to start over at Neal, and my time at Southern. I remembered kneeling in front of the little church, weeping over my family situation. Years of insecurities, years of pain, and years of inner turmoil, and now finally this realization: I belonged.

My conversation with "Big Al" was the final confirmation for me.

# CHAPTER 19

## JUST PERFECT

Don Larsen was at best an average Major League pitcher who bounced around the big leagues, pitching for eight different teams in 14 years and ending his career with a losing record. While pitching for the Baltimore Orioles in 1954, he lost 21 games. They traded him to the New York Yankees in 1955, and in 1956, Larsen started Game 2 of the World Series against the Brooklyn Dodgers, sent to the showers in the second inning after giving up six runs. After such an ugly outing, he was convinced he would not see action again in that series. Amazingly, he found out hours before Game 5 that he would be the starting pitcher for that pivotal matchup with the series tied 2-2. When the game ended on October 8th, 1956, Larsen had faced 27 batters and retired them all. 27 up … 27 down.

Perfection. It had never happened before in Major League Baseball postseason play and has not happened since.

In 2007, the New England Patriots had a team for the ages. Tom Brady, the GOAT (Greatest Of All Time) quarterback, threw a then record 50 touchdown passes, and Hall of Fame wide receiver Randy Moss had 23 touchdown receptions, a record that still stands. The Patriots set numerous offensive records on their way to an undefeated regular season record of 16-0. New England was the heavy favorite in Super Bowl XLII to defeat the New York Giants and cap off the first perfect season since the Miami Dolphins' mythical run in 1972. Against all odds, the Giants scored with only 39 seconds left for an improbable 17-14 victory over a team that looked invincible.

Perfection for the Patriots was so close, but they came up 39 seconds short and failed to seal the deal.

The COVID-19 virus reared its ugly head in 2020 and caused death, displacement, and disruption. One of the many sports casualties was the 2020 NCAA Basketball Tournament. With the virus lingering in 2021, it was a minor miracle that the NCAA tournament could be completed that year. The talk of the 2020-2021 season was the Gonzaga Bulldogs, who destroyed every opponent they faced during the regular season in record-setting fashion. They were the heavy favorite to win the title. After waltzing through their first four tournament games to gain a spot in the Final Four, it looked like they would become the first NCAA basketball team since Bobby Knight's Indiana Hoosiers all the way back in 1976 to finish undefeated. In the title game, however, their quest for perfection ended with a loss to Baylor.

Why has it been almost 70 years since an MLB player has thrown a perfect game in the postseason? Why is it now approaching the 50th anniversary of the only undefeated NFL team in the Super Bowl era? Why has no NCAA men's basketball team since 1976 finished unbeaten?

Perfection. Persistently pursued. Rarely realized.

Could the '83 Spartans finish their regular season undefeated for the first time in school history? Could we complete that elusive perfect season? We were 6-0 and realistically had only one team left on our schedule with a legitimate shot at beating us. Apex High was our Week 7 opponent, and they were the surprise of the league that year. After finishing with a dismal 1-9 record the previous year, the Cougars were off to a 3-1 start in conference play, led by junior running back Rex

Hawley. After his third consecutive 200-yard rushing performance, Hawley was getting attention statewide. The trip to Apex to square off with the Cougars would definitely be a test, with Al Carson saying he almost made this game his upset pick of the week. He predicted Southern by 3 in overtime.[36]

Apex proved to be a tough opponent, but we were finally finding our rhythm offensively after losing Stanley, and we had 431 total yards, 24 first downs, and scored almost at will in a 40-19 conquest of the Cougars. Darryl again had a big game, rushing 33 times for 224 yards, pushing him across the 1,000-yard mark for the second straight season, and also scored three touchdowns. Coach Davis heaped praise upon Darryl, as our bruising fullback rushed for 200-yards for a second consecutive game. "I swear, McGill is awesome. He ran over people. He hurt people. He makes things happen when he puts his hands on the ball. If there's a better running back in the state, I'll have to see him. The longer the game goes, the stronger he gets. And everybody we've played has used a nine-man front against us. He gets into a rhythm, and he's ready for anything."[37]

It was also becoming apparent that our offensive line was very special. Even though we typically only used a handful of plays from our playbook each week and teams often knew what was coming, they still couldn't stop us. Although Darryl was a special back, Coach Davis wanted to make it known that he was running behind one of the best high school lines that North Carolina had ever seen. "Let's give credit to the offensive line. Mike McClure (C), Mack McClure (TE), Kevin Sowell (T), Tommy Upchurch (G), Duke Thomas (G), Arthur Wiggins (T), Todd Wright (TE), and David Andrews (TE). They keep blowing people off the ball. These kids have worked hard all season. They're experienced, and they know they can make it happen. They see it. These kids are very confident, and these kids got some skill." Apex coach Bruce Worley summed up the impressive strength of our line. "They took it to us. And in the second half, they wore us down. I can't say enough about McGill, but even I wouldn't mind running behind a line like theirs."[38]

Coach was also proud again of our defense, as we utilized the Double-Will linebacker again and Stacey started opposite of me. In an interview after the game, Coach Davis pointed to both Stacey and me, impressed with the way we were able to limit Hawley and the Apex running game. "I don't know how Bazen keeps doing it."[39] Although I had gotten a lot of credit after the East Wake game for helping limit their star receiver, I thought the coaches were the key. Our coaches always seemed to put us in the right position, and their decision to go with two Will linebackers again this week was spot on.

Coach Davis realized the significance of this win, as we equaled a school record set in 1979 with our seventh straight win. He seemed downright giddy after the game. "I'm so proud of our kids. How about that? 7-0!" There are no givens in sports, but with our final three regular-season games against the conference cellar dwellers, it appeared that this team would certainly rewrite the school record book.

An interesting moment in the game occurred with one minute to go in the third quarter. Apex had scored to cut our lead to 27-13, and we quickly drove down the field. On first and 10 from the Cougars' 24, Coach finally called a play we practiced each week but had yet to run: flanker right post, belly left fake, bootleg right pass. I would split out wide to the right and when the ball was snapped, I would take a 45-degree angle path towards the safety, as if I was going to block him. Randy would fake the ball to Darryl on our bread-and-butter play, belly-left, give-to-the-full. We ran this play so often that it would draw the attention of the entire defense to that side of the field. Our tailback would also go to the left side of the field as if he would get an option pitch. With all the motion moving left, at the last moment Randy would pull the ball from Darryl's stomach, hide it on his right hip, and spin back to his right. At the same time, I would plant my left foot, change directions, and now do a 45-degree post to the right corner of the end zone. The play worked just as we had often practiced, leaving me wide open in the end zone, no defender within 15 yards. It was an easy throw for Randy, and his perfect pass was easy to reel in for the touchdown. I began to celebrate until I saw the yellow flag on the field, wiping out my first touchdown of the season. One of our linemen was flagged for being too far downfield, and the play was called back. Most importantly, we had now run this play in a game situation, and it was clear it could be our ace in the hole.

The next month was a blur. We had a week off, helping us to rest our bruised and battered bodies, then it was time to finish the task of an unbeaten regular season. Week 8 was Homecoming, and we punished Western Harnett 45-6. The next week's victim was the other Harnett County  school, Harnett Central, and we recorded our second shutout of the season in a 63-0 demolition that could have been much worse. In this game, we set school records for most points in a game and largest margin of victory.

Finally, we faced off with crosstown rival Jordan with our perfect season once again on the line. The Falcons had denied perfection to our jayvee team on this same field two years earlier, but we left no doubt this year in a 45-7 drubbing of our nemesis. With the score 38-7 and our second unit in the game, we had the ball on Jordan's 10-yard line with two minutes to go. I thought my night was over until I heard Coach call my name.

"Tony, get in there for Clint and tell Brent to run 23 Dive."

"Yes, Sir!" I responded and pulled my helmet down upon my head as I sprinted on the field. I relayed the play to Brent, who was now leading our second unit. I would be the two back on this play and run the ball through the three-hole between our left offensive guard and left tackle. On first down, Brent handed me the ball, and I found a small hole and squeezed through for six yards. Coach screamed out for us to run the same play again. On second down from the Jordan four-yard line, I took the handoff and struggled ahead for three yards. The clock had ticked down inside one minute, and it was now third and goal from the one.

"Give the ball to Tony. Same play!" Coach yelled out. On the third attempt, the left side of our line opened a massive hole, and I was able to basically walk into the end zone. Not counting the touchdown against Apex that had been negated by a penalty, it was my first touchdown of the year and our team's last in a perfect regular season.

Although Darryl once again stole all the headlines with 234 yards rushing and five touchdowns, it was a total team triumph, with the Spartan machine firing on all cylinders. Randy only threw three passes but completed all of them, including a 28-yard touchdown pass to Antuane. The defense was dominant as usual, holding the Falcon to seven first downs and a meager 101 yards of total offense. Charles Lee had a big game with a fumble recovery and a blocked punt. The defense would have recorded our third shutout of the season if not for Jordan employing an illegal play, the Lazy End where a player steps on the field right before the snap of the ball. Coach Davis reminded reporters that the Spartans were not a one-man show. "It's been a whole team effort all season. No one individual stands over the team."[40]

And what a team this was! Darryl was posting video game numbers each week, with five straight 200-yard rushing performances, 1,829 rushing yards for the season, and 31 touchdowns, all school records. Our massive offensive line was manhandling opposing teams, opening gaps for him to run through. Our defense had really come into its own and had become as dominant as our offense, totally shutting down each offense we faced. Jordan coach Hal Keith, whose team had faced undefeated crosstown city rival Northern High School earlier in the season, had this to say, "They're as good as any team that we've played."[41]

As the final seconds ticked off and the horn sounded, ending the contest, we gathered in the end zone. There was a feeling of satisfaction that is difficult to explain. We had avenged our loss on this field from two years earlier. We had extended our school-record winning streak to 10 games. We had just put an exclamation point on the first unbeaten regular season in school history. We were the top-ranked and highest-scoring team in the state. We were the odds-on favorite to win the state title. On a personal level, I had not only been on the team this year, but I was also a starter. Miraculously, although I was the smallest guy on the team, I was leading the team in tackles. I had just scored my first touchdown of the season. I had an exclusive interview this year with "Big Al." I had a beautiful girlfriend whose family genuinely liked me. I would drive her cool Camaro the whole weekend. I belonged. I was important. I was a Southern Spartan!

On November 4th, 1983, at 9:45 pm on the football field at Jordan High, everything seemed just perfect.

# CHAPTER 20
## GAME DAY

Game day mornings are something that only football players can really comprehend. All of these days were special, but this day had much more significance, as our game was getting the most coverage statewide. In an unlucky twist of fate, our first-round opponent was not a first-round tune-up against an outmatched opponent but a matchup with a formidable foe. The Clinton High School Dark Horses had a storied football program, annually one of North Carolina's top teams. This year was no different, as the Dark Horses also sported a 10-0 record and were only a few spots behind us in the AP rankings, checking in as the #4 ranked team in the state. Both teams were conference champs, both were undefeated, and both were highly ranked. No wonder reporters from around the state would fill our press box that night, eager to get the scoop on this important game.

"It's a normal Clinton ball club," Coach Davis told reporters in the lead-up to the game. "They've got talent, a good coaching staff, and tradition. This is the way it should be. When you get into the playoffs, you should play a championship-caliber football team. I'm looking forward to it." [42]

In another twist of fate, our first-round playoff game coincided with Veterans Day, so school was out for this national holiday. The coaches, ostensibly to keep us in a somewhat normal routine, decided that we should be at school by 9:00 that morning. Some of us were convinced that our coaches, aware that we had many team members who liked to party, wanted to keep our team out of the weed(s). The coaches informed us that they would have some special pregame activities lined up for us and that also we would be treated to a special meal.

Even though we didn't have to be at school until 9:00, I still woke up at 6:00 and immediately mentally rehearsed the day. I took a shower, thankful at this moment that Angela and Billy were no longer at home and Brenda took her shower at night, meaning that I had enough hot water today for a long shower. I took advantage of this luxury and waited until the last drop of really hot water was gone before getting all the soap off my body. I got dressed, grabbed *The Durham Morning Herald*, ate a big bowl of cereal, brushed my teeth, and then waited for Adam.

In the lead-up to the big game, Coach Davis reminded championship-starved Spartan supporters of all that this terrific team had already accomplished. Southern fielded its first varsity team way back in 1955, and this team was the first to ever go through the regular season unscathed. "The pressure is off my back. Ten and 0 is tough for anybody in this day and age. So many things come at you. This is just super. No matter what happens in the playoffs, nobody can take this away from us."[43] This team had indeed made school history, but none of us wanted to rest on our laurels; we all wanted that state championship ring.

Wearing my white jersey with the big red "47" on the front and back and my only pair of jeans, I waited for the trusty Orange VW to make its way down my dusty, scarcely graveled road, and roll into my driveway. We always wore our football jerseys to school on game days, donning the white jersey that year for away games and our fiery red one for home games. There was the usual small talk between Adam and me on the 15-minute ride to Southern, but my mind was already a million miles away. I was immersed in game strategy, replaying in my head over and over what we had practiced all week. This day. This game. This moment. There seemed to be no doubt in my mind as we drove the familiar route to school that the next 15 hours would be the most important in my life to that point.

There was a team meeting at 9:00 in which Coach outlined the schedule for the day. I mentioned earlier that Rocky III had been a hit movie the year before and that *Eye of the Tiger* had been our school band's favorite song to play during games. The coaches had secured a VHS of the inspirational movie, and the plan was to view it together as a team and then to go eat lunch at Bullock's Bar-B-Cue. Everyone seemed excited about the special meal, although we remembered that the basketball team was treated to steaks the previous year during their playoff run. We were not as excited about having to show up early and watch the movie. After watching Rocky defeat Clubber Lang, it was time for us to load up on the bus and go eat lunch.

On the way there, the mood was light as Adam, Stacey, and I quoted our favorite parts of the movie.

Stacey started the show with his best impersonation of Clubber Lang, aka Mr. T, a new actor sporting a distinctive Mohawk whose performance in this movie made him a household name. "No, I don't hate Balboa. But, I pity the fool."

Adam, taking the role of Rocky, did his best imitation of a fight scene between Balboa and Lang. "You ain't so bad; you ain't so bad; you ain't nothin'. C'mon, champ, hit me in the face! My mom hits harder than you!"

It was Stacey's turn again, now sounding more and more like Mr. T. "I'm the baddest man in the world. I'll beat you like a dog, a dog, you fool!"

Stacey and I mimicked the exchange between the interviewer and Lang, as I took the role of the reporter and held up my fisted hand in front of my friend as an imaginary mic.

Interviewer: "What's your prediction for the fight?"

Clubber Lang: "My prediction?"

Interviewer: "Yes, your prediction."

Clubber Lang: "Pain!"

Then I ended to show with Apollo Creed's admonition to Rocky, "There is no tomorrow. There is no tomorrow."

For this team and this dream, there was no tomorrow.

Bullock's Bar-B-Cue had been a must-eat restaurant in Durham since 1952, the longest-running restaurant in the history of the city according to their website. Their specialty, of course, was their signature barbecue, but they were also known for their Brunswick stew, fried chicken, and delicious hush puppies. For me, this was a special treat. Going out to eat was a rare occurrence in my family growing up. On rare occasions when we had this privilege, we were far more likely to find ourselves beneath the Golden Arches of McDonald's or eating like royalty at Burger King. I savored every bite of this meal, not knowing that for us it was more than lunch; it was the Last Supper.

We laughed, ate, laughed some more, ate dessert, and finally boarded our bus to head back to Southern. We were encouraged to rest for an hour in the afternoon and later the parents had arranged for food to be brought in for a light dinner before the game. Before we knew it, it was time to walk to the field house and get dressed for the big game.

While getting dressed that night, there was a quietness in our locker room that was almost eerie. We were the top-ranked team in the state. Our school and community were counting on us to bring home a title. Were we finally starting to feel the pressure from the weight of these expectations? After putting our uniforms on, we all sat on the benches in front of our lockers, waiting to go out on the field to stretch, go through some simple warm-up drills, and then go to battle. Before going outside into the cool, windy, drizzly November night, Coach Davis gave us one last pep talk.

"This has already been a special year, one that none of us will ever forget. You guys have put in the work, and the result is the best team in school history. But we're not done yet. If we play Spartan football tonight, we won't be beat. The sportswriters think we're the best team in the state. Our fans think we're the best. I think we're the best team. Tonight, let's go out there and leave no doubt! Now everyone get in here!"

We huddled closely together, said the Lord's prayer as a team, and lined up to step onto the stage, actors about to take part in a tragedy.

# CHAPTER 21

## DARK HORSE

What is a dark horse? This refers to someone previously unknown or lesser known that suddenly comes to the forefront of a competition. A dark horse is an underdog, someone that on paper has little or no chance to win.

I'm not sure exactly how Clinton High chose the Dark Horse as their official school mascot, but the definition certainly didn't match their football program. Since World War II, the football team had endured only two losing seasons. Dark Horse coach Bobby Robinson presided over an absolute football dynasty in eastern North Carolina, entering the game with a career record of 113-28 and just finishing the third of what would be four straight 10-0 regular seasons. Robinson was 2-0 against Coach Davis and Southern, knocking us out of the playoffs in 1974. Clinton may have been called the Dark Horses, but they were not a dark horse.

Although not an unknown with little hope for victory, Clinton was a decided underdog against us. They were a good team; we were a great team. They had some talented high school players; we had Division I talent across our roster. They had a talented running back in Lennie Faison, who entered the game with 1,110 yards; we had one of the best running backs in the nation, who had already tallied 1,829 yards. This was our game to lose, as they say.

So, when we won the toss and elected to receive the opening kickoff, we fully expected to win. Clinton kicker W.F. Spell teed up the ball and prepared to kick as Darryl and I took our deep positions in our kickoff return alignment. W.F. Spell. I will never forget him. I will never forget that name. He was a chunky kid who looked like he had a love affair with hamburgers. Unlike the trend of the day of soccer-style kicking, Spell still used the two-step, straight-ahead strategy to boot the ball. I never found out what W.F. stood for, but I will never forget this guy or his name.

Coach had called for us to run a reverse to the right side of the field on this kickoff. I stood to the right of Darryl, and if I caught the ball, I would immediately run parallel to my left and hand the ball to him on a reverse to the right. Darryl lined up on the left, and if he caught the ball, he would start to his right and fake a reverse to me. The point was simple: get the ball in Darryl's hands. The ball came directly to me as I stood on our 10-yard line; I caught it cleanly and started to my left. I met Darryl right in the middle of the field and handed him the ball. Off Darryl galloped down the right sideline, making it all the way to our 40 before being pushed out of bounds. This was an impressive start, hopefully a sign of things to come.

As we broke the huddle for our first down play, Kevin noticed it immediately. "Unbalanced line! Unbalanced line!" he screamed out. Clinton had done a masterful job of scouting us, and they knew we had stacked our best blockers on the left side of the line. They had slid their defensive alignment that way and had placed an additional defender in the off-tackle gap between Kevin and Mac. With an extra man on that side of the ball, it would make the going tough on that side all night.

We liked to begin games with the tried-and-true belly-left, give-to-the-full. Upchurch would pull from his guard position and block the defensive end. The wingback on the left side would fill the gap left by the pulling guard, blocking the unsuspecting defensive lineman. Mac and Kevin would block down, pushing the defense inside, usually leaving a massive hole for Darryl to run through. This game was no different, as we called

Darryl's number again. Clinton was ready, and the extra defender on that side left us outnumbered. They hit Darryl at the line of scrimmage, driving him back for no gain. Second and 10.

"They're lining up guys in all the gaps and have slid an extra linebacker to this side of the ball," Mac said, a hint of concern in his voice. "How we gonna block that extra man?"

"We all gotta communicate when we get to the line. Call a man. Tell each other who ya got." Mike demanded.

Kevin encouraged the super seven on the line. "We've got this! Just like all year. No one can stop us."

Randy called the play. "I-left, 21 Dive. I-left, 21 Dive. Ready … break!" This was a quick handoff to me through the one hole, the gap between the center and left guard. "Down …. Set … Hut 1!" Randy called out the signals and then took the snap from Mike. Randy then took one step to his left and handed me the ball, and I immediately ran into a wall of white jerseys, gaining only one yard.

"There's a man in every gap," an exasperated Upchurch said in the huddle. "They're stacking the line and overloading this side. We can't block 'em all."

Third and nine from our 41-yard line. "Tony, Tony!" I looked up and saw Antuane running towards the huddle, holding up his right arm as he called my name. This was the signal that he would take my place. He gave Randy the play, and Randy looked in the eyes of the 10 young men standing in front of him and said, "Flanker right, belly left fake, option left."

Randy took the snap, faked a handoff to Darryl, and went around the left end with the option to keep the ball himself or pitch it to Antuane, who was trailing him. The Clinton defense crashed hard on our quarterback, forcing him to pitch the ball to Antuane, who tried to take the ball around the left end but was stopped after a four-yard gain. Fourth and five, and we were forced to do something we rarely did the entire year: punt the football. There were several games during the year when our punter, Mac, never booted one punt. Maybe it was nerves, perhaps it was caused by lack of opportunities in game situations, or maybe the ball was wet because of the soggy field, but whatever the cause, something happened that was a bad omen of things to come.

As Mike, our long snapper, was hiking the ball to his brother Mac, it came up one yard short, bouncing about crazily past his twin and taking off downfield. Mac chased the ball as it bounded further and further in the wrong direction, deeper and deeper into our territory. When he finally caught up with the ball and tried to run, the Dark Horse defense corralled him all the way back at our 13-yard line.

I ran onto the field with our defense, a strange feeling growing in the pit of my stomach, but still confident. With our offense leading the state in scoring and with Darryl's running rampage through our conference, the defense had not gotten the attention we deserved. We had recorded two shutouts and only gave up an average of 7.3 points each game. Even though our offense got off to a slow start, our D could rise to the occasion.

On first down from the 13, Clinton ran up the middle, and the running back was met in the hole by Mike, a collision loud enough to hear high above in the press box. Mike stood over the dazed ball carrier, now lying prostrate on the turf, and taunted him. "All night long, baby! All night long! We got a lot more where that came from!" Second and nine from the 12. The Dark Horse offense lined up again in their wishbone formation with 3 running backs behind the quarterback, and this time tried a misdirection run off tackle. Cheeseburger fought off a double team block and met the back in the hole, and when he fell forward for a two-yard gain, it was now third down and seven from our 10-yard line.

Mac encouraged us in the defensive huddle. "Third down. One more stop. C'mon y'all. Hold 'em!"

On this crucial play, Clinton again used misdirection, and their running back found some room around the right end. He almost broke completely free before Jay from his cornerback position could bring him down on the three-yard line. Did they have enough for the first down? The chain gang, led by Karen's father Paul, came out for the measurement. We made eye contact as he passed by me, and his facial message seemed to say, "It's ok. You guys are better than they are. Take a deep breath." When they stretched out the chains, Clinton had a first down by inches.

Clinton now had four chances from the three-yard line to score the game's first points. The first down play was a handoff up the middle, and again the interior of our defense was up to the challenge. Mac and Kevin hit the running back simultaneously, stopping him for no gain. Second and goal from the three. The second down play was a pitch around the left side, where I was in my two by two alignment behind our defensive end. Their elusive running back took the pitch and sped toward the corner of the end zone. He got outside our end and was about to get the corner on me as well when I dove for his legs, catching his ankle and bringing him down at the one-yard line. Third and goal.

In the huddle, Mac gave us instructions for this huge play. "Goal-line, slant right! Goal-line, slant right! Ready. Break!" Darryl was also a great defensive player and came in for Brent at safety in our goal line alignment.

At the snap, all the defenders slanted right, and Darryl and Mac crashed through the middle of the line. The Dark Horse quarterback executed a perfect fake to the right to the fullback, who was absolutely obliterated by our Darryl and Mac, then turned quickly and handed the ball on the left side to the wingback. He waltzed into the end zone for the score. W.F. Spell, that guy again, attempted the extra point, but Darryl leaped high and got a hand on the kick, sending the ball off to the right of the goalpost.

After the failed extra point attempt, I looked back at the scoreboard and saw a very unusual sight. For the first time all season, we were trailing on the scoreboard. Visitors -6, Southern -0. No time to panic. There were still three minutes left in the first quarter. The game was still early. Gut check time. Time to show what we were made of.

We took the kickoff from W.F. Spell and returned it to our 33-yard line. In the huddle, there was an increased urgency from everyone. "Let's take the ball and run it down their throats," Mike said. "Run belly-left again, and I promise Mac and me will open a hole for Darryl," Kevin said with an intensity that caused his eyes to spit fire. Randy called the play. "I-left, belly-left, give-to-the-full."

We ran to the line, angry at being behind and wanting to reclaim the lead as soon as possible. Darryl took the handoff and found a gap off tackle, as Kevin had kept his promise with Mac and him blowing the Clinton defenders off the ball. Darryl was finally dragged down after a seven-yard gain. "That's what I'm talking about!" said Kevin. "That's Spartan football, boys!" shouted Mac. "This is our game!" Upchurch said with fervor. Second and three from the 40. Randy called the play. "21 Fake, Crossbuck left." Randy would fake a handoff to me on the left side of the center and then hand the ball to Alan Tilley on the right side of the center. Darryl also went to the left side of the line, and with everyone following his every movement, the fake to the left worked perfectly, leaving Alan with a big opening on the right side. He was stopped after a 10-yard gain, giving us a first down on the 50-yard line.

"They can't stop us!" Duke yelled, celebrating the huge hole he had helped open on the right side of the line. "This is our game!" cried a confident Cheeseburger. He was a mainstay on our defensive line, but after Arthur Wiggins was injured towards the end of the year, Vincent was now thrust into action full-time at right tackle on offense as well. "Give me the ball!" demanded Darryl. "I'll take it to the house." The coaches sent in the play. Bread-and-butter time again. I left, belly-left, give-to-the-full.

The ball was snapped, and our line surged forward with a vengeance, clearing a path for our remarkable running back. Darryl hit the hole at full speed and ran untouched 50 yards to the end zone. I had filled the gap left by Upchurch when he pulled to block the defensive end, and when I collided with the defensive tackle, the jolt sent me to the ground on my backside. I had done my job, however, as I kept him away from Darryl, and I watched the big white 44 on his jersey get smaller and smaller as he sprinted for pay dirt. I got up and sprinted the 50 yards to enjoy this moment with the team, and as we celebrated our first touchdown, there was a deafening roar from the crowd. There was an almost tangible electricity in the stands, and an experience like this made all the years of hard work that it took to get here seem worth it. This was high-stakes high school football at its best. Friday night lights before Friday Night Lights. And I was smack dab in the middle of it.

Mike Wiggins came on the field for the extra point. Wigg would have battled for a starting position at offensive guard and handled our extra points, but he was injured early in the season and missed seven games. He didn't have a powerful leg, but he was deadly accurate from 20 yards or closer. His extra points were usually straight through the middle and would barely clear the goalposts, but he was usually money on these. While he was out for so long, we had Cheeseburger attempt some extra points, but although he had a much stronger leg, he was not nearly as accurate. We could use Cheese for field goals, but we went the entire regular season without attempting even one. Why settle for a field goal when you could just score touchdowns? The ball was snapped to the holder, Brent Farrell, who placed it down. Wiggins stepped forward and booted the ball straight through the middle, giving us a 7-6 lead with roughly a minute to play in the first quarter.

Old Mo, the crazy sports phenomenon better known as momentum, seemed clearly on our side now. The early deficit seemed to shake off whatever cobwebs we had from the movie and meal earlier in the day, and everyone was fired up. We kicked off, and our 11-man army like a swarm of killer bees attacked the poor guy who fielded Cheeseburger's long kickoff, knocking him rudely to the ground at his own 22. After their first play netted them only two yards, the first quarter ended with us on top 7-6.

The second quarter started well, as we held Clinton short of a first down, forcing them to punt. They wisely chose to punt the ball away from Darryl, and it bounded out of bounds on our 39-yard line. It was now that I made a mistake that seemed to choke the life out of our momentum, and it's a play that still haunts me to this day. We ran 23 Dive, which was simply a straight handoff to me running in the gap between left guard and left tackle. The ball was snapped, and I exploded from my three-point stance through the hole as Randy placed the ball in my arms. I've never seen so much open space, as Upchurch and Kevin had cleared a wide swath for me, and their safety had followed the fake to Darryl on the left end. My eyes opened wide, as it appeared that I had a clear path to the end zone.

I never saw it coming. From out of nowhere, a Dark Horse defender hit me from the side like a heat-seeking missile hitting its target perfectly, his helmet directly on the ball. When his helmet reached its intended destination, the ball squirted out from its position in my right arm, and as the defender drove me violently to the turf, the ball was now laying on the ground like a big brown egg about to be pounced on by a bunch of basket-carrying boys at Easter. The big Clinton middle linebacker had blindsided me, and as he lay on me with his full weight pressing me to the earth like a tack holding a thin paper in corkboard, I reached futilely for the pigskin prize, but it was just out of my grasp. My very spirit was crushed when a Dark Horse defender pounced on the ball, and his teammates began to whoop and holler around him, looking at the prize pig he had snared. It was *Lord of the Flies*, my favorite book in high school, all over again. I was now like Simon in that book, the skinny, quiet kid who was thrown to the ground and stabbed repeatedly by the crazed mob, only I lay prostrate on the grass, each scream of joy a new kick to my soul by the devilish Dark Horses.

A forever memory that I cannot shake is that of lying face down on the muddy, soggy turf as the realization of what had just happened plunged deeply into my heart. I remember staying there for what seemed like days, pounding my fists repeatedly into the muck and mire, incredulous at what just happened. I had not carried the ball that often over my 10 years of playing football, maybe a total of 100 times in all. Although somewhat of a small sample size, I had never fumbled the ball. Never. Until now. How could this happen at this moment? The weight of letting my team down threatened to sink me completely beneath the quagmire that our field was becoming with each passing moment, until I was rescued by a massive arm that pulled me like a rag doll to my feet. It was Kevin, and his words helped bring me back to reality. "Shake it off, TB. We're still in the lead. Forget about it. We'll get the ball back."

When you play both offense and defense, there was little time to sulk over your mistakes. In a flash, I was in our defensive huddle, trying to listen to the defensive call and get my head back in the game. If we could hold them on this drive and get the ball back, I would feel much better about my blunder. If they scored on this possession, I would feel responsible. To my dismay, Clinton embarked on their only sustained drive of the game, and 10 plays later they covered the final eight yards of this 49-yard drive. When the Dark Horse wingback crossed the goal line and Clinton regained the lead, I began to have this gnawing fear that this might not be our night. W.F. Spell lined up for the extra point, Darryl soared high into the air again to block the kick, but this time the ball sidestepped his outstretched hands and barely made it over the goalpost, giving the boys in white a 13-7 lead.

The kickoff return team huddled up on the sidelines, but my mind was not on the next play. I was still thinking about the mistake from 11 plays earlier. Had I fumbled away the game and our shot at a state title and a perfect season? If we never regained the lead, I would never be able to live with the guilt. Thankfully, Old Mo is a fickle fellow, and just as swiftly as we lost momentum, we snatched it back.

Our next drive got off to a rough start, as Darryl fielded the kickoff and slipped in the mud, his knee touching down on our own 20-yard line. I rarely said anything in the huddle, but if I didn't speak this time, I would burst into tears. "It's my fault we're behind. I'm sorry, guys."

Upchurch tried to help me refocus. "That's in the past. We'll pick you up."

Darryl spoke to us all. "Just give me the ball. We are not going to lose this game."

Coach gave Darryl the ball and on first down, he found a hole and barreled ahead for a big 23-yard gain. He got up and beat his right hand across his chest. "Now that's what I'm talking about!"

"That's Spartan football, boys!" Coach yelled from the sidelines. "This is our game. Let's run it down their throats."

And we did exactly that. We blew the Dark Horse defenders off the ball, and in 6 plays, we had first and goal on the one-yard line. Coach called belly left fake, option left. Randy would fake the handoff to Darryl and then roll around the end with the option to keep it himself or pitch it to the tailback. Inside the ten-yard line, Randy had kept the ball and run it in himself all year, and he did the same once again, running untouched into the end zone to tie the game at 13-13. When Wiggins booted the extra point through the uprights, we had a 14-13 lead. Little did anyone know that this would be the last touchdown either team would score.

I felt so much better. I had made a crucial mistake, but my team had my back. With a few minutes to go before halftime, we were leading.

I breathed a deep sigh of relief. Clinton had one last possession before intermission, and we needed to make sure they didn't put any more points on the board. The Dark Horse offense moved the ball to the 50 with under two minutes to go before the break, and their quarterback rolled to his right to attempt a pass. I took my 45-degree angle drop into the short coverage zone and saw a white shirt flash to my right. Clinton's QB rifled a pass to the receiver who had done a circle route behind me, evidently not seeing the red jersey with #47 on it, and I was able to take one step to my left, jump high into the air, and intercept the pass. There was nothing but green grass in front of me, a clear path to the end zone. Unbelievably, fate seemed to frown on us again. When I landed, I was missing a shoe. I somehow jumped out of my right cleat, landing awkwardly and now trying to run with only one shoe on. After hobbling forward for five yards, I was brought to the ground at the Clinton 48. Jay was in deep coverage behind me on that play, and he later said, "I remember Tony's interception and him coming out of his shoe, or I think he would have scored." In 10 years of organized football, I never lost a shoe. Why did it happen now? We weren't able to move the ball on our first two plays, and the clock ran out on the first half.

Redemption of a sort for me. Earlier in the quarter, I fumbled away our momentum but then also snagged an interception. As a team, we had suffered adversity yet still led at the half. We were clearly the better team, as we had outgained Clinton handily. Their two scores came off our turnovers, and if we cleaned up our mistakes, we would be fine. This was the message Coach Davis had for us at the half.

"Take a deep breath, boys. We made some mistakes we don't normally make, but we are still in the lead. They can't stop us on offense; we've only stopped ourselves. We'll kick off to them to start the 3rd quarter, get a three and out, and then get the ball and drive it right down the field. We are the better team. Now let's go out there and finish this thing."

Two twelve-minute quarters left in the game. Just 24 minutes. We didn't know it as we exited our field house into the now drizzly, windy night and returned to the increasingly swampy field, but we had only 24 minutes left in our season. Just 1,440 seconds to be more precise. I always wondered if we knew how short our time was, would we have played the last half any differently? Similar to our life, we have a limited period of time left on life's scoreboard clock. One day, the last second will tick off, and our final gun will sound. If we knew how little time we had left in life, would we be inclined to live life differently?

The third quarter followed Coach's instructions to a tee. Almost. Cheeseburger booted the second-half kickoff deep into Dark Horse territory, and our coverage team stopped the runner at the 27. Clinton ran three plays that only netted six yards, forcing them to punt. Their punt was a good one, hitting the sod at the 30 and finally resting at the 16. From there, we began THE DRIVE.

On January 11th, 1987, John Elway led his Denver Broncos on a 15 play, 98-yard drive to break the heart of the Cleveland Browns. This memorable masterpiece became known as simply The Drive. Our version of a long, methodical drive to break the will of an opponent predated Mr. Elway's. It was also 15 plays but a little shorter in length at 76 yards. It was a thing of beauty. All the way until the end. Then it became ugly.

The Drive was a perfect microcosm of our '83 offense. All except for Play 15.

The first 14 plays of The Drive were textbook Spartan football. Nothing fancy. No frills. Just smash mouth football. There were the regular heaping helpings of Big Macs, those continual belly-left and belly-right handoffs to Darryl that were gut punches to opposing defenses. There was also a new dish served up on The Drive. Alan Tilley, a talented sophomore who had been called up from the jayvee after Stanley's injury, ran the ball multiple times on this drive. Darryl, as normal, led the team in rushing that night with 121 yards, but Allen was our secret weapon, rushing 13 times for 56 yards. Clinton did a great job scouting ways to stop Darryl, but they had little tape on AT, and he rose to the challenge that night, especially on this pulsating drive.

There were no big gainers, just four yards here, another 3 yards here, and many third and short-yardage situations that we converted. The well-oiled Spartan machine drove methodically down the field, an unstoppable force, a rerun that Southern supporters enjoyed watching over and over. After the first half scare of being behind for the first time, there was a collective sigh of relief in the stands with each yard that we chewed up on The Drive. We would score, kick the extra point, go up by eight, and then our defense would shut the door on the Dark Horse dreams of defeating us. Our fans had seen this movie before. Play 15 of The Drive, however, brought an ending with a tragic twist.

There are different views of what actually happened on second and goal from the 6-yard line. Charles Chandler, from way up in the press box, saw it this way. "Quarterback Randy Leathers rolled to his right and pitched out to running back Antuane Simmons. However, the ball slipped through Simmons' hands."[44] Chandler was spot on with most of his analysis of Play 15, as Randy did roll to his right and pitch the ball to Antuane. His perspective of the play was skewed, however, by the height of the press box and the angle from which he viewed the action. He used a plural word in his description, *hands*, that was completely inaccurate. His depiction of the play pins the blame on Antuane, as if Randy gave him a perfect pitch that he fumbled away. It was an innocent mistake by the writer, but one that made Simmons a scapegoat.

Play 15 took place on the Home side of the field and very close to the sidelines. Antuane had himself brought this play in from the sidelines and took my spot in the huddle. As was normal, when I came off the field, I would stand beside Coach Davis on the sideline, waiting to shuttle in the next play. We were as far down the sideline as the rules allowed, standing on the 25-yard line, and I had a bird's-eye view of what transpired. We were in our I- right formation, and Randy took the snap and rolled to his right. Antuane stayed in his proper alignment as the pitch man on an option play, keeping a distance of about five yards behind the quarterback and positioned at a 45-degree angle. Another fact worth noting is that Antuane had enormous hands, perhaps the largest I ever saw on a high school player, earning the nickname HANDZ from one of our coaches. Randy indeed rolled to his right, and he did pitch the ball to Antuane, but the ball was NOT fumbled by the young man with the big hands. The ball did NOT slip through his hands, as he only was able to get one hand on the ball. When Randy rolled right and decided to pitch the ball, his pitch was behind Antuane, forcing him to plant his right foot and stop on a dime and lunge back to his left, his body almost parallel to the ground. The pitch was so errant that even after stopping and diving back to his left, Antuane was still only able to get ONE hand on the football, his left hand, and the ball went bounding away in the opposite direction of the end zone.

Play 15 only got worse from here as Clinton corralled the pigskin and the tide of the game completely turned. From where I was standing, everything seemed to move in slow motion. The ball was spinning around near the sidelines on the 10-yard line, before a Dark Horse defender named Preacher Williams picked up the ball and started the other way with nothing but green grass in front of him. As he raced down the sidelines, Kevin Sowell somehow chased him down and dove towards him, contacting him just enough to make him step out of bounds on the 40.

What happened on Play 15? Was it a fumble by our running back? Was it a bad pitch by our quarterback? Was a Clinton Preacher pronouncing judgment on us for some collective discretion in our past? Mike McClure had a far more nefarious explanation. "Randy changed the play. The ball was supposed to go to Darryl on belly-left, and he changed the call. He audibled at the line of scrimmage. That wasn't the play Coach called." Mike is correct about the play that was sent in from the sideline. What did Randy see that caused him to change the play?

This play sucked the life out of the stadium and our team. Instead of preparing to plant a dagger in the Dark Horse dreams, we were now knocked back on our heels, and Clinton had great field position to start their drive as the third period wound down. We held Clinton to eight yards on their first three plays, but on third down they pulled a play out of their bag of tricks, handing the ball to a running back who ran to his right and then handing it back to the end on a reverse to the left. The play caught us off-guard, as we were in an all-out blitz, and by the time we stopped the ball carrier, Clinton was in business with a first down inside our 20 as the third quarter clock hit zero.

When the third quarter gun sounded, it was our tradition to hold four fingers high in the air and scream out, "4th Quarter! 4th Quarter!" It was now the final quarter, and we still had the lead, but there was a definite cloud of uneasiness that had enveloped Spartan Stadium. First and 10 from the 13, and our dreams were on the line. The defense huddled up.

"We must hold them here. Give it all ya got!" Mac pleaded.

"We've come too far to lose now," Kevin reminded us. "It's still our game. They will not get in the end zone. Let's shut the door on them now!"

And shut the door we did. Three running plays netted eight yards, and Clinton faced a big decision on fourth and two from the five-yard line. To our surprise, W.F. Spell, who was also their offensive tackle, lined up from the left hash mark to attempt a field goal that, if successful, would put them in front. What an unlikely scenario here. No one all year had attempted a field goal against us, and we had not attempted a field goal either. So that guy again, W.F. Spell, lined up from the left hash with the odds stacked against him. It was a difficult angle, and now he would be kicking into a strong wind.

The ball was snapped. We surged forward. W.F. Spell stepped toward the ball. Darryl leaped high into the air. I couldn't rush the kicker because I had pass coverage responsibilities in case of a fake kick, so I was trapped on the edge, helpless to do anything but watch as the ball sailed through the air and barely cleared the uprights. I turned and looked at the big scoreboard, which was directly behind us on this end of the field. It now read Clinton 16, Southern 14. There were 10:02 seconds left to play.

We received the kickoff and began to move quickly down the field. We had a first down at the 50 when things stalled. Three plays netted only 5 yards, leaving us with fourth and five from the Clinton 45. Our fourth-down play was unsuccessful, leaving only seven minutes on the clock. It was time for the defense to stand strong as they had all year, and we were up to the challenge. We stuffed three straight Dark Horse runs and forced a punt. They punted away from Darryl again, and the ball bounced out of bounds at the 34 with 5:19 remaining on the clock. It would be our last offensive possession of the year, so it was desperation time now.

We moved at a frantic pace, running the ball five straight times to get us to the Clinton 49 with just under three minutes remaining but now faced a fourth and five. Randy dropped back to pass and found Mac on a down-and-out route for a 12-yard gain, giving us a fresh set of downs on the 37. The clock was ticking, so we wasted no time.

Alan subbed in for me, and we huddled up quickly and called two plays. The first down was a handoff to Alan for a gain of three yards. "Back to the line!" shouted Randy. "Everybody on the ball!" We handed it off quickly to Alan again, who this time found a crease in the defense for five yards. Third and two.

The clock was now our enemy, each second that ticked off like a knife to the heart of our chances. We needed a first down desperately, so Darryl's number was called. He didn't fail to deliver, dragging two defenders ahead for a four-yard gain and a first down at the 27. We called our second time out, leaving us with one, to catch our breath and plot our strategy. Randy ran to the sideline where I stood beside Coach Davis, and Coach mapped out the next play.

Coach calmly talked to Randy as I stood there incredulous at the play he called. "Here's the play. Flanker right post, belly-left fake, bootleg right pass. Carry out the fake. The play will work. Tony will be open." Randy made eye contact with me, but no words were exchanged. Did he disagree with the play call? Did he not have confidence in me?

We had run the play just once all year in the Apex game, and I caught the pass. When Randy got the instructions, he turned and jogged back to the huddle. I took off for the huddle as well, longing to run alongside our quarterback as we prepared to run this all-so important play. Just hoping for that nod of encouragement or some affirmation that he believed that I could do this.

Back in the huddle, Randy called the play. "Flanker right post, belly-left fake, bootleg right pass. Flanker right post, belly-left fake, bootleg right pass. Ready. Break!"

We made our way to the line. Everyone did their job. Darryl and Randy carried out their fake to perfection. Everyone moved left and then at the last moment Randy pulled the ball from Darryl's stomach, put it on his hip, and spun back to his right. The line blocked, giving our quarterback time. I ran the route as I had practiced many times, heading straight for the safety as if to block him and then running my post to the right corner of the end zone. The play could not have gone any better, and I found myself alone in the right corner of the end zone. There was not a Dark Horse defender within 20 yards.

With one minute to go in the biggest game of the season, alone in the end zone waiting for the pass that could change history, was the ultimate dark horse.

# CHAPTER 22

## TO PASS OR NOT TO PASS

Alone. This was the familiar feeling on the playground many years earlier in kindergarten. I remember this fear of being alone when I got on the bus on the first day of school at Neal. I had felt this feeling so many times when getting off the school bus at the top of Pineview Drive, knowing that my parents would be working. This is the feeling I would sometimes get even in the midst of a crowd of people. Alone.

If there was ever a good time to be alone, it was now. If ever a play had worked exactly as drawn up, it was this one. There I was, two yards deep in the end zone, ten yards from the sideline, in perfect position to catch THE PASS. All I had to do now was catch what was sure to be a perfectly thrown pass by Randy. I wasn't nervous about this, as this was the one skill with which I felt very confident. If a count had been kept over all these years of how many times a football had been thrown my way and I caught it, it would surely number in the millions. Countless times while in my front yard, I threw the ball high in the air and caught it myself. Literally tens of thousands of catches were made on my parent's king-size bed when they weren't home. I would throw the Nerf football way out in front of myself, forcing me to dive on their bed to make miraculous catch after miraculous catch. All the catches from passes thrown by Timmy Brewer, as we would practice catching the ball and keeping our feet inbounds. I had prepared all my life for THIS PASS. This was a done deal. I would catch the pass. No sweat. I was just waiting. And watching.

To my horror, for some reason still unknown, Randy decided not to follow the script. The play that called for a pass to me. The play that had been executed perfectly. The play that had placed me wide open in the end zone only about 35 yards from where Randy stood in the pocket. The play that could have given us victory and continued our dream season. Unbelievably. Inexplicably. Randy decided not to execute the play. Randy did NOT throw the ball.

Randy decided to run the ball, and he was tackled for no gain. I stood dumbfounded in the solitude of the end zone, trying to comprehend what had just happened. From 35 yards away, I stared angrily at my boyhood idol. Why, Randy? If it was some personal thing between you and me, don't punish the team. Why, Randy? You would have still gotten the glory. You would have thrown the winning touchdown pass. Why, Randy? Why couldn't you just run the stinking play? Trust the coaches. Why, Randy? You may have other chances playing at the next level, but this is it for most of your teammates. Why, Randy? Why didn't you throw the ball?

Charles Chandler wrote about this play in *The Herald* the next day. "Southern then missed out on an excellent opportunity to score. On first down from the 27, Southern coaches called for a misdirection pass play to Tony Bazen. Bazen's pass route worked to perfection, leaving him open in the right corner of the end zone. However, Leathers chose to run on the play and was tackled for no gain."[45]

This wasn't the last play, but for all intents and purposes, it was our last best chance. We had to quickly call our last timeout after Randy's run, leaving us now with no way to stop the clock. On second down, Randy connected with Antuane for a five-yard gain to make it third and five from the 22. We then had Darryl run a circle route out of the backfield, and he found a seam in the defense. Randy's pass was high and barely grazed the top of Darryl's fingers as he attempted to make the catch. It was now fourth down and five from the 22 with only 46 ticks left on the clock. Decision time for Coach Davis. Instead of trying for a first down or touchdown, we heard Coach begin to yell at Cheeseburger, "Field goal! Field goal! Get your shoe on!"

We were out of timeouts. There was no time to take a breath and think it over. There was a mad scramble to find the square-toed cleat, and a general sense of panic overwhelmed our sideline as the play clock was winding down. A five-yard delay of game penalty would have made kicking a field goal even that much more difficult, so a desperate search ensued for that shoe. Tony Thomas finally located the missing object, threw it to Cheeseburger on the field, who hurriedly tried to take off his regular cleat and replace it with the specially designed shoe. We had to rush to line up, Cheeseburger barely had time to get in position, and he slipped on the wet turf as he stepped forward to kick. His 40-yard field goal attempt fell way short, the Dark Horses took over and ran out the clock, and our dream season was over. Just like that.

I recall watching the final seconds disappear from the scoreboard clock, and when the gun sounded signaling the end of the game, it felt like a rifle shot to my heart at point-blank range. I don't remember shaking hands with Clinton. I don't remember walking off the field. It was all like a bad dream that my mind blocked out. When I regained conscious memory, I was sitting on the floor in our field house in front of my shiny red locker. As I looked around, no one was sitting on the benches; everyone was planted on the floor just like me. We typically removed our equipment quickly after games, showered, and dressed for the festivities to follow. Not one person for 10 minutes dared take off any portion of their beloved SHS uniform. With no movement in the room, the only sound was that of 31 young men weeping unashamedly.

I admire Coach for how he kept his composure at a time that I'm sure he just wanted to sit and weep with us. Instead, he circled the locker room and one by one spoke to each of us, consoled us, and hugged us. Then he spoke to the entire family. "I've never been prouder of a team than I am of you. Don't hang your heads. You have so much to be proud of. This was the best team in the history of the school. You have a place in history and will never be forgotten. You seniors will graduate soon and will go on to lead families. I hope that you can take lessons that you learned as a player here and become the best men you can be. I love each and every one of you, and it's been my privilege to be your coach. Now get changed and walk out of here with your heads held high."

We followed his instructions and slowly began to remove all of our equipment. For most of us, tonight would be the last time we took off our armor. As I unbuckled my shoulder pads and slipped them over my head, it was this realization that stung the most.

We took refuge in our locker room for a long time, not wanting to face friends, family, and fans we felt we had disappointed. Coach Davis did not have this luxury as there was a horde of reporters waiting to pounce on him with questions, wanting to know how his Super Team lost. Our head coach left us in the care of the assistant coaches and went to face the music. As always, he was classy in his responses. "This was the best football team we've had here. It's a shame for the kids that it had to end like this. It was a super year. We just couldn't seem to cut out the little mistakes tonight. How do you explain fumbles? Take out the miscues ... I know you can't do that. It's all part of the game. I appreciate what the kids did for Southern. They gave us a great effort all season and a great effort tonight."[46]

In 2021, after 10 of the members of this team connected from literally all around the globe for a Zoom meeting, Charles Lee summarized what all of us felt that night. "We were young and thought we knew so much. We thought it would never end. I don't think any of us realized what a special time it was until it was too late, and the season was over." Tommy Upchurch and I started playing organized football at Bethesda many years earlier and knowing that this part of our lives was now gone cut like a knife. "Since football was such a big part of my life, those guys were pretty much my family. I remember crying when I got home after that loss in the state playoffs. It wasn't from the loss of the game but the realization I'd never play football with those guys again." Even though so much time has passed, the pain of that loss still feels as real as it did that cold November evening in 1983. When asked about his memories of that defeat, Jay was candid in his response. "I still have a sour taste in my mouth almost 40 years later. I've never been able to watch film of that game."

If the game film was watched, it would show that one team was clearly superior to the other. The final statistics show that we dominated the game in every way. We outgained Clinton 310-179 and had a 15-8 edge in first downs. We also held an almost two-to-one edge in time of possession. We beat them in every category except the one that mattered the most: the final score. 16-14. I will *always* hate this combination of numbers.

Veterans Day. Friday, November 11th, 1983. A day that will always live in infamy for Spartan players, coaches, and fans.

There were no physical casualties that day on the SHS battlefield. There were, however, many hopes and dreams that died.

# CHAPTER 23

## THE AFTERMATH

Several years ago, I came across this soul-searching poem that at first glance seemed to encapsulate our '83 football team and the incredible missed opportunity that still troubles me almost 40 years later.

*Mr. Meant-to has a comrade.*
*His name is Didn't-Do.*
*Have you ever chanced to meet them?*
*Have they ever called on you?*
*The two live together*
*In a house called Never-Win.*
*And I'm told that it is haunted*
*By the Ghost of Might Have Been.*

Then there are the words found in John Greenleaf Whittier's poem *Maud Muller*, "For of all sad words of tongue or pen, the saddest are these: '*It might have been!*'"

What might have been if my grandfather had not gone to confront the father of the boy who bullied my dad? What might have been if my dad had not had a drinking problem? What might have been if we stayed on Jones Circle and I attended Lowes Grove instead of Neal? What might have been if Stanley had not gotten injured? What might have been if

Randy had thrown me the ball? What might have been if we had beaten Clinton?

I spoke with Mike McClure in May of 2021, the day after he welcomed his ninth grandchild into the world. He still lived in the southern part of Durham, not far from where he grew up. He had some health issues, partially related to all those years of football, but he was happy with his lot in life. "The way my life is now, I wouldn't change it. I love my wife. I love my children. I have all these grandchildren." His dad pushed Mac and him to play sports … to be the best. After so many years of the grind of training year-round and the pressure to excel, Mike and Mac finally had their fill. The twins who seemed born to play football, maybe even at the professional level, walked away from a plethora of scholarship offers and hung up their cleats for good after the Clinton game.

"We had college offers," Mike recalled. "Back then they would offer you cars, houses, money, girls. I enjoyed football, but then it became a job. In high school, when everyone else was on summer vacation having a good time, my dad made us go to Duke and practice with their football team. Other people were at the beach, and we were in Durham, hitting college football players. It didn't matter how many people I put out, like the Jordan game, when I knocked four out of the game and sent one to the hospital. It was never enough for my dad. Football became just a job."

Mike never pushed his three children to play sports, but athletics was in their genes. Mike's son Robert, a 6-2, 330-pound lineman, followed in his dad's footsteps and was a standout player at Southern. Unlike his father, he chose to play football at the next level, actually earning the ring that eluded dad when Fayetteville State University won the CIAA championship in 2009. His son Chance was a basketball standout at SHS before transferring to South Granville. Despite their natural athletic prowess, Mike decided to let them find their own way, choosing to stand in the background and cheer them on. "I didn't want to end up like my dad," he said.

Even though Mike had been blessed with a large family and was at peace with himself, he was still haunted by the missed opportunity way back in 1983. He had many questions about particular plays in the playoff game that just didn't seem to add up. He had known for years about Randy's drug issues, as both had played varsity since Grade 10. While sophomores playing on the varsity, there were seniors on that team who made crack available at the back of the bus, according to Mike. "I knew what was going on, but I never went back there." By Grade 10, however, Randy had already developed the habit that would eventually send his life into a downward spiral. Mike said the rumors about what really happened in the Clinton game started shortly after that nightmare November night, and Randy himself fueled the fire. "When he would get high, he would tell the story."

Was there more than meets the eye regarding that playoff game? What really happened at Southern High School on November 11th, 1983? Mike speaks with absolute certainty about the reason this team of a generation could not deliver Coach Davis and Southern High their first state title.

What story did Randy tell others, according to Mike McClure? "Everyone had the feeling that Randy threw the game. There were a lot of bets placed on the game. Randy was on cocaine and owed some people a whole lot of money. We had the best high school offensive line there's ever been in North Carolina. We had the best running back. I know he threw the game. Everybody knew it. He didn't want to win. His heart was somewhere else. Randy threw the game. Yes, he did."

Numerous players have believed for years that our star quarterback gift wrapped the game for Clinton. Kevin said he knew something was off with Randy that night. "I just think about that game replaying it in my head, and I just knew he was not there. He was not doing the regular things that he would do to win. I thought that Randy threw the game even before it came out as a rumor." Antuane had heard how well that our opponent had prepared for us, but he believed that would not have mattered if not for #12's puzzling play. "Clinton could've scouted us forever. It wouldn't have made a difference if Randy had played his game. I can vividly recall four separate plays that if Leathers had done what he normally did, we would've scored a touchdown. Four separate plays. He definitely played like he threw the game." Antuane pointed to several plays where the play called for Randy to pass, and he had wide-open receivers, but chose to run the ball instead. It just made no sense to many observers. We rarely aired it out, and, on several plays, a pass was called; the line blocked perfectly giving Randy time to deliver the throw, the receivers' routes left them open, and yet the ball was not thrown.

Antuane concluded by sharing some thoughts that numerous teammates have echoed. "I'd love for someone to get to the very bottom of what was going on with our senior quarterback, Randy Leathers, in that playoff game. If Randy could open up and tell us the truth about that night, or if some coaches or teammates who may have some insight as to what was going on with Randy that night could fill the world in on the truth, then we'll have the answer to why this 1983 Southern Durham football team was not crowned the NC 3-A State Champions."

Several teammates heard that Randy was so high on drugs against Clinton that it affected his play. Another teammate had heard that this was the only game the entire season that Randy wasn't under the influence of drugs and wasn't accustomed to playing when he wasn't wasted. There was talk of a cocaine-fueled after-party following the loss in which "the coke was crazy, and Randy was acting like we won." There is so much talk is out there that it is hard to separate fact from fiction, and the passage of time makes it even more difficult as memories get blurred.

I also talked to Coach Davis in May 2021. His body had been weakened by a stroke the year before, but his mind was still as sharp as a tack, able to recall intricate details of his early career at SHS. His memories of our '83 team were as fresh as the morning dew. "That was a great group. The McClure boys. Mike and Mac were tough. We had McGill. That was a special team. If we hadn't been so selfish, especially at quarterback, we probably could have won it all."

What did he mean by selfishness possibly costing the team a title? There was one play in particular in that climatic Clinton contest that still troubled Coach. "We were up just by a little and were driving to put the game away. I told Randy to hand the ball to Darryl. I told him not to pitch it. He pitched it anyway, and it went behind Antuane. They picked it up and almost ran it back. Randy decided for some reason or another to pitch it. I guess he wanted to be the star."

I asked Coach if over the years he became aware of the rumors that our quarterback had thrown the game. He was philosophical in his response. "I heard something about it later. There's nothing that can be done about it now. You can't cry over spilt milk. You just have to go on with life."

Life indeed went on for Coach Davis after the '83 campaign, but I've always wondered if he ever completely got over that missed opportunity. He coached one more season at Southern then took a sabbatical from the sidelines for many years, finally resurfacing in 1991 at Durham Riverside, a new school. He started the program there without a senior class and had them in the playoffs by year three. Coach Davis later was Head Coach at Forbush and an assistant at Tarboro before retiring in 2001. He got the coaching itch again in 2006 and briefly came out of retirement to guide the ship at Smith High School in Greensboro, a post he held for just a short time before health issues forced him from the sidelines permanently.

Monty Davis won countless conference titles, had multiple playoff appearances, was selected Coach of the Year several times, coached in the Shrine Bowl, and is certainly high on the list of the best high school coaches in North Carolina history without a state title. He should be wearing a ring that has 1983 NC 3-A State Champions inscribed on the back. Why is that particular piece of jewelry missing from our coach's hand?

Was it just selfishness or something more that derailed us on our path to perfection? Mike concluded our conversation with these words. "Remember this, man. You lived a movie. There are all these movies about people throwing a game because they owe someone money. All these movies about drugs interfering with sports, but we lived the movie in real life. We can't get it back. It's gone now. *Think of what it could have been*."

So many questions for which we will never have answers. When faced with the "*What might have beens*" of life, we have two options: We can wallow in our "what ifs" and live a life of discouragement, despair, and defeat, or we can pick up the pieces of any broken circumstance and keep moving forward. I decided long ago not to live out my years lost in life's rearview mirror, but instead to focus my attention on the front windshield and the infinite possibilities that exist. Not having closure, however, makes moving on more difficult.

It is certain that Randy became addicted to drugs in high school and eventually spent much of his adult life in prison after committing several armed robberies. What is not certain is whether or not this addiction in high school led him to do the unthinkable, something that would break a cardinal rule of athletics, purposely losing a game. I reconnected with him, and eventually, the conversation turned to that team … that season … that game. "I'm still haunted by that pitch, but Antuane did get his hand on it," Randy remarked, as if years later trying to reconcile in his own mind what happened.

I asked Randy if he remembered our conversation from many years earlier when he visited me at Louisburg College and told me something that shook me to my very core. A little over a year after graduation from Southern, Randy traveled to Louisburg, NC, and we went out that evening with some friends. During the course of the evening, when we were alone at our table, Randy told me a story about drugs, debts, gambling, and a fixed game. I was incredulous, and told Adam Finch, my college roommate, when I returned to the dorm that night. Randy's "admission" that night has never left me, and I asked him about it shortly before his 55th birthday in May 2021.

His reply was simple but seemed sincere. "I don't remember meeting you at the college. I don't remember going out to eat with you. Because of the drugs, I don't remember much from that time. I really told you that I lost the game on purpose and got paid off? That's quite a story right there for sure. I was probably just trying to come up with something big. I may have told you that, but I promise you that it didn't happen."

Did Randy owe money to drug dealers, get desperate, and pay his debt by throwing the playoff game? Did he ignore play calls, refuse to throw to open receivers, and pitch the ball behind Antuane all on purpose, or did he just pick a bad game to have a bad game? How much of a factor, if at all, did drugs play in the outcome of the game? We may never truly know the answer to these questions.

To add more fuel to the conspiracy theories that seem forever attached to this game, this disturbing news appeared in *The Durham Morning Herald* in the spring of 1984. "Southern High football followers certainly remember the Spartans' loss to Clinton in the first round of the 1983 state 3-A playoffs. Southern entered the game ranked number one in the state, but it seems that the Dark Horses had a distinct advantage. Clinton's coaches were unable to use their walkie-talkies because Southern's coaches were using the same frequency. However, Clinton was able to pick up the communication between the Southern coaches in the press box and on the field. 'We knew every play they were going to run,' a Clinton coach said recently."

Years before Coach Bill Belichick and the New England Patriots were found guilty of both Spygate and Deflategate, did Clinton Coach Robinson and his staff pull off Radiogate? Months after the game, Charles Lee asked Coach Davis about the Walkie-Talkie Warfare that took place during our playoff game. "He said he knew about the radios being on the same channel, but Clinton agreed to turn theirs off at halftime. 'Clinton wasn't listening to our radios,' Coach Davis said. I just rolled my eyes and walked away."

If Clinton admitted to cheating in the first half, could we really trust them to turn off the radios after halftime? Even if the dirty Dark Horses decided to play fair in the second half, how much damage did their indiscretions cause in the first two quarters? If a Clinton coach admitted to listening in on our radio communications and stealing our plays, should they have been sanctioned for their actions?

What is truth, and what is fiction? Why did this dream season end prematurely? After seeing and experiencing so many things through the years, I believe I have discovered the answer.

The reason we lost that playoff game was not because of Randy, not because of Stanley's injury, not because of my fumble, not because Clinton cheated, not because of the wet field, nor an errant punt snap or bad pitch. We lost the game because *it just wasn't meant to be*. Just like it wasn't meant to be for that Grade 9 Lowes Grove team to finish undefeated. Just like it wasn't meant to be for our Grade 10 jayvee team to win the last game in the rain at Jordan to cap a perfect season. No blame. No pointing fingers. Just the realization that some things are not meant to be. We can muddle through life mired in the muck of *Might Have Been* or we can just rest in the realization of *Not Meant to Be*.

The cliché is true, "It's not how you start; it's how you finish." My dad had a rough start, experienced some struggles, and made some mistakes along the way, but he finished well. The same man who told me as a 10-year-old that there was no God met Him on this side of eternity a few years before he died. For the last five years of my dad's life, he was truly a new man. What AA, New Year's resolutions, and countless attempts at self-reformation could not do, a relationship with Jesus did. For the first time in 50 years, my father lived life as a sober man. We reconnected, forged a strong bond, and when I was 38, I heard my dad say "I love you" for the first time. He finished well.

Randy did have a good start, hit some speed bumps along the way, and like so many of us, got off track. While doing time in a Colorado prison, he committed his life to Christ, and it was more than jailhouse religion. Speaking with him now is to talk with a man who has found inner peace and true contentment. He is devoted to his daughters and volunteers time at local AA meetings to encourage and mentor men that struggle with some of the same demons that he was finally able to slay. Randy was always a leader who was looked up to and is now using those leadership skills in a powerful way. And once again, others look up to him. Randy is trying to finish well.

Whether Randy had a bad game against Clinton or put the game in the bag for them, he is still family. Just like we rallied around Tony Thomas after the Jordan game in tenth grade, we should rally around our quarterback. Just like Spanky stepped in when Jay was in the fight of his life against Orange High, we should step in and help Randy in his fight to stay clean. Just like Kevin pulled me off the muddy turf after my fumble in the playoff game, we should pick Randy up.

I heard years ago that God is the God of the Second Chance. I respectfully disagree with this. God is NOT the God of the Second Chance; He is the God of ANOTHER CHANCE. The truth is that I have dropped the ball in life far more than once and have needed more than a second chance. Every time in life that I have messed up, disappointed others, and been less than what I should be, there is a God who has always offered forgiveness, a fresh start, and another chance. If God is willing to give people another chance, we should do the same. After all these years, we should do all we can to help our quarterback finish strong.

I didn't have the best start in life. I didn't catch the winning pass. I wasn't carried off the field, and I wasn't able to secure an athletic scholarship, but I have lived as full a life as I could hope for. I did get an academic scholarship and became the first in my family to graduate from college. I am father to two wonderful daughters, Rebecca and Bethany, whose heart for helping others is a continual source of joy. I have been privileged to teach and coach some amazing students and have sought to impact them in the same manner that my teachers and coaches did in my life. I have written music, worked as a sportswriter, wrote for a national magazine, served in ministry, and literally traveled the world. I write these words from Beijing, China where I have worked as a school principal for a number of years. I am married to a beautiful Chinese woman, not my first girlfriend Janna but an amazing, inspiring jewel named Shirly.

No, I didn't have the best start or the easiest path, but I also want to finish strong.

In 2019, Shirly and I traveled to North Carolina to visit family and friends. I took her on a tour of the life of Tony Bazen. Our first stop was the small house on Farthing Street, the first home I remember. We then traveled to Jones Circle and saw the brick house with the carport. Finally, we drove from the Bethesda community to Oak Grove to our old place on Pineview Drive. So many memories wrapped up in these homes and these neighborhoods.

Then I wanted her to see the schools I attended. I wanted to show her East End Elementary, but this school where I attended Kindergarten had long since been closed, the building purchased years ago by a church. I took her to Bethesda, where I spent six years of my life. Not much had changed with the school or the Athletic Park. Then we made the trek to Baptist Road to the site of Neal Junior High, where I spent three important years in grades 7-9. The facilities looked much the same, but the school is now Neal Middle School and houses grades 6-8.

Finally, we drove to 1818 Ellis Road, the site of "Old" Southern High School, where I grew into a young man, graduated, and the place that fateful football game took place. The Old Southern was located in Research Triangle Park, and the site became more and more valuable as tech industries continued to flood into the area. In 1993, Glaxo pharmaceuticals company arranged with Durham Public Schools to provide a replacement campus and purchased 84 acres on 800 Clayton Road for the "New" Southern High School to be built.

Southern not only has a new address; it has a new name: Southern School of Energy and Sustainability. Racial demographics have changed. Out of the 1,255 students that walked the hallways in the 2020-2021 school year, 52% were African American, 40.6% were Hispanic, 3.2% were two or more races, and only 3.3% were white.[47] It's mindboggling to think that a school once nicknamed the Rebels, that was all-white, and that proudly flew the Confederate flag has undergone such a metamorphosis in the last 50 years. What transpired at Southern during my generation is a microcosm of the transformation that occurred in Durham. Izzy Jensen gave an amazingly accurate summation of the new Bull City that has emerged from the ashes of its past. "Durham has changed from a small town behind the times, resisting change and holding onto racist ideals to a progressive and inclusive city. Like it has in the past, it today has a responsibility to be an example for the rest of the country and to show that, even in an ex-Confederate state, we can find peace and prosperity between people of all races and ethnicities."[48]

This racial peace and prosperity in Durham have been far more than 50 years in the making. From being home to some of the only profitable African American businesses in the country during the late 1900s, earning Parrish Street in downtown Durham the title of the "Black Wall Street," to the founding of North Carolina Central University in 1910 as the first public liberal arts college for African Americans, to Duke University making the decision to desegregate four years before the Higher Education Act mandated it, Durham was in many ways a little ahead of the curve in the race for racial equality. This race, obviously, is far from over.

That's why when a young black football player spent the night at the home of a white teammate and shared a bowl of cereal the next morning, there was a question of what to do with the bowl. That's why the use of a certain racial epithet has not been eradicated from the vocabulary of all Durhamites. That's why in 2019 white students accounted for only 19% of total students in the 53 Durham Public Schools as the rise of charter schools and an exodus to private schools has led to what has been termed resegregation.[49] There is still much work to be doe.

*2018 SHS Spartans*

Old Southern and New Southern are strikingly symbolic of Old Durham and New Durham. To think this evolution took place slowly before our eyes, almost imperceptibly as everyone was so busy living life, hits me in the face every time I'm back home. In some ways, however, this old saying rings loud and clear: the more things change, the more things remain the same. The constant through the years that has helped bridge two campuses and very diverse student populations has been football. The football fervor that Monty Davis brought to SHS way back in 1968 has yet to subside, and although the boys in red and white are now mainly black and brown, Fall Friday nights on 800 Clayton Road still unite a community like little else can.

Our city changed. Our school changed. Each player on the '83 team ... we learned ... we grew ... we stumbled and fell ... we got back up. We changed. Ultimately, for the better.

My Durham kindergarten burnt to the ground by the fires of racism. Selfishness scorched the state title hopes of our '83 team. My childhood charred by alcoholism. But all three rose from the ashes.

Our '83 dream season that had a nightmarish end created a hunger for that elusive state title. It was not until 2003, twenty years after our special season, that another Southern football team rose through the ranks to be voted the top team in the state. These Spartans were 13-0, #1, and like us, favored to win the school its first state title. The 2003 season also ended with a bitter taste when they were upset in the state semifinals. Heartbreak again.

Southern's insatiable thirst for a title was exacerbated in 1993 and again in 2010 when city rivals Northern (1993) and Hillside (2010) won North Carolina 4A State Championships, the first and only football titles for each school. Would the Spartans ever bring home the ultimate prize?

It took 30 years, but in 2013 SHS finally completed the job that seemed to be the birthright of the '83 squad, capturing the school's first state title. The Spartans were finally state football champions!

Yes, things have changed at Southern, but be sure to be there for the last home football game. Follow the Spartans as they exit the field for the final time. Notice the young boy (his skin may be brown or black now) with his face pressed against the fence, marveling at the size of the varsity players and dreaming of one day wearing the red and white. He calls out for a memento from his heroes, hoping for an arm pad, an elbow pad, a chin strap, a wristband ... or even a used mouthpiece.

# EPILOGUE

**M**onty Davis decided to leave Southern after he completed his seventeenth season as Head Coach. The '84 team that followed us was special as it was the last at Southern for this coaching legend. The 1984-1985 Southern High School yearbook was dedicated to him, and the words on this page were poignant. "Eighteen years ago, there was a small football team at Southern High School that was not very well known. The next year the Southern football team got a new coach. This coach began to work his magic, and there was a dramatic improvement in the performance of the team. For seventeen years, Coach Monty Davis has worked his 'magic' on the Southern High School football team. He has helped make our team very well known. Other teams look at our team with respect and admiration. Not only other teams, but the Southern football players look on Coach Davis with respect and admiration. The team members tease him with the nickname 'Taz,' but some have said that he is 'a superb leader,' not only in athletics but also in his business classes. This school is really going to miss the 'magic' of Coach Davis."[50]

**Darryl McGill** was selected to the All City-County Team, All-Conference Team, All-Area Team, All-State Team, and was chosen as the All-Area Back of the Year and 1983 N.C. Player of the Year. He was selected to play in the Shrine Bowl that pitted the best players from NC against the best from South Carolina. Coach Davis summed up Darryl's career at Southern. "I've been in coaching for 19 years, but I've never had a back quite like Darryl. He's a rare kid… probably the best to come out of the Durham area in a long time. There are other backs around who probably have more speed, and there might be some backs who can cut a little better -though I don't know where -but I don't think anybody combines all those qualities like Darryl."[51] He received a scholarship to Wake Forest University and was a 4-year letterman. He led the Atlantic Coast Conference in touchdowns in 1986 with 11. He was drafted by the Washington Redskins in 1988, but his career was cut short by a knee injury. The World League of American Football (WLAF) was founded in 1990 and lasted one season. In 1991, he played for the Raleigh-Durham Skyhawks. Darryl currently resides in Tampa, Florida.

**Mike McClure** was selected to the All City-County Team on offense and defense, All-Conference Team on offense and defense, All-Area Team, was chosen All-Area Lineman of the Year, was named to the All-State Team on offense, and was selected to play in the Shrine Bowl. He turned down numerous scholarship offers and stayed in Durham, where he resides today. For years, he worked in the Heat and Air Conditioning industry.

**Mac McClure** was selected to the All City-County Team as a tight end and linebacker, All-Conference Team on offense and defense, All-Area Team Honorable Mention, and was All-State Honorable Mention. He turned down numerous scholarship offers and stayed in the Durham area. For years, he worked in the carpet industry, owning his own company. Today he battles back and knee problems.

**Kevin Sowell** was selected to the All City-County Team as an offensive lineman and linebacker, All-Conference Team on offense and defense, All-Area First Team on offense and Honorable Mention on defense, and All-State Team on offense. He played football at Western Carolina University. He was a law enforcement officer and member of the SWAT team near Atlanta, Georgia for many years before retiring in 2021. Kevin said, "One of my proudest moments in life was being a part of the '83 team."

**Vincent Ford** was selected to the All City-County Team, All-Conference Team, and All-Area Team. He accepted a scholarship to play football at East Carolina University. He worked in the banking industry in Charlotte for many years but had a lifelong love affair with his hometown of Durham, which he visited often.

**Brent Ferrell** was selected to the All City-County Team, All-Conference Team, and All-Area Team.

**Antuane Simmons** was selected to the All-Conference Second Team and All-Area Honorable Mention in 1983. In his senior year in 1984, he received numerous accolades and played football at East Carolina University. He served in the North Carolina Army National Guard for over 33 years, reaching the rank of First Sergeant (1SG), and seeing active duty in Iraq and Kuwait.

**Randy Leathers** was selected to the All City-County Team, All-Conference Team, and was All-Area Honorable Mention. After high school graduation, he attempted to walk on to the football and baseball teams at Western Carolina.

**Tommy Upchurch** was chosen All-Conference Second Team and All-Area Honorable Mention.

**Todd Wright** started at tight end in 1983 but was moved to offensive guard his senior year. He earned numerous honors in 1984, including being selected to the Shrine Bowl. He went to Elon College after graduation, choosing baseball over football.

**Arthur Wiggins** started at offensive tackle in 1983. He was a standout on the '84 SHS team and played football at Elon College.

**Stacey Winston** joined the Army and served for eight years, stationed at Ft. Bliss, Texas, Ft. Bragg in Fayetteville, NC, and also in West Germany. He worked 18 years at Goodyear Tire and Rubber Company. Wrestling was his first love, and he started his own wrestling club, the College Lakes Juggernauts.

**Tony Bazen** was named to the All City-County Team, All-Conference Second Team, All-Area Team Honorable Mention, and received the Golden Helmet Award as the Spartans' Most Inspirational Player.

# REFERENCES

1   "African-American History." *Discover Durham*, www.discoverdurham.com/community-culture/black-history/durhams-story/.

2   Carrier, Sarah. "Malcolm X Debates Floyd McKissick in 1963." *NC Miscellany*, 24 June 2017, blogs.lib.unc.edu/ncm/2017/06/24/malcolm-x-debates-floyd-mckissick-in-1963/.

3   Carson, Al. "Just How Good Are the '83 Spartans?" *The Durham Sun*, 22 Aug. 1983, pp. 2-D.

4   "Southern Foursome Draws Notice." *The Durham Sun*, 10 July 1983.

5   "Southern Foursome Draws Notice." The *Durham Sun*, 10 July 1983.

6   Carson, Al. "Just How Good Are the '83 Spartans?" *The Durham Morning Herald*, 22 Aug. 1983, pp. 2-D.

7   Carson, Al. "Worth the Price." *The Durham Sun*, 19 Aug. 1983.

8   Carson, Al. "Just How Good Are the '83 Spartans?" *The Durham Sun*, 22 Aug. 1983, pp. 2-D.

9   *1983 Southern High Spartans Football Program*, Aug. 1983.

10  "7-0, Spartans Romp." *The Durham Sun*, 8 Oct. 1983.

11  Chandler, Charles. "Sowell's Towel Wiping Smiles Off Foes Faces." *The Durham Morning Herald*, 25 Oct. 1983.

12  Chandler, Charles. "Southern Notes." *The Durham Morning Herald*, 28 Aug. 1983.

13   *1983 Southern High Spartans Football Program*, Aug. 1983.

14   "The Crack Epidemic - The History of Crack Cocaine - Drug-Free World." *Foundation for a Drug-Free World*, www.drugfreeworld.org/ drugfacts/crackcocaine/a-short-history.html.

15   "Spartans Favored in Football." *The Durham Morning Herald*, 26 Aug. 1983.

16   Chandler, Charles. "Southern's Run, Pass Rip Orange." *The Durham Morning Herald*, 27 Aug. 1983.

17   Chandler, Charles. "Southern Notes." *The Durham Morning Herald*, 28 Aug. 1983.

18   Chandler, Charles. "Spartans Un-Dunn Over '82 Loss To Wave." *The Durham Morning Herald*, 2 Sept. 1983.

19   "Southern Spartans Stun Dunn." *The Durham Sun*, 3 Sept. 1983.

20   "Southern Ranked No. 1 in High School 3-A Poll." *The Durham Morning Herald*, 5 Sept. 1983.

21   Carson, Al. "Spartans Lose Faison, but Stay Unbeaten." *The Durham Sun*, 12 Sept. 1983.

22   Chandler, Charles. "Faison's Injury Big Blow for Southern." *The Durham Morning Herald*, 9 Sept. 1983.

23   Carson, Al. "Prep Notes." *The Durham Sun*, 15 Sept. 1983.

24   Carson, Al. "Northern, Southern to Stay Unbeaten?" *The Durham Sun*, 16 Sept. 1983.

25   Chandler, Charles. "Southern Turns Over Webb, 28-0." *The Durham Morning Herald*, 17 Sept. 1983.

26   "Hillside High School (Durham, North Carolina)." *Wikipedia*, Wikimedia Foundation, 8 Apr. 2021, en.wikipedia.org/wiki/ Hillside_High_School_(Durham,_North_Carolina).

27   Chandler, Charles. "Southern, Hillisde Collide In Inaugural Football Game." *The Durham Morning Herald*, 23 Sept. 1983.

28 Carson, Al. "McGill, Spartans Overcome Fired-up Hillside." *The Durham Sun*, 24 Sept. 1983.

29 "Discover the Story of EnglishMore than 600,000 Words, over a Thousand Years." *Home : Oxford English Dictionary*, www.oed.com/.

30 Chandler, Charles. "Southern-East Wake Generating Attention." *The Durham Morning Herald*, 30 Sept. 1983.

31 Chandler, Charles. "Prep Notes." *The Durham Morning Herald*, 2 Oct. 1983.

32 Carson, Al. "Spartans Blitz Warriors." *The Durham Sun*, 1 Oct. 1983.

33 Chandler, Charles. "Spartans Down East Wake." *The Durham Morning Herald*, 1 Oct. 1983.

34 Elmore, Grady. "So. Durham Rips Warriors." *News and Observer*, 1 Oct. 1983.

35 Chandler, Charles. "Prep Notes." *The Durham Morning Herald*, 2 Oct. 1983.

36 Carson, Al. "Prep Notes." *The Durham Sun*, 7 Oct. 1983.

37 Britt, Tony. "Southern Tops Apex, 40-19, Behind McGill." *The Durham Morning Herald*, 8 Oct. 1983.

38 Britt, Tony. "Southern Tops Apex, 40-19, Behind McGill." *The Durham Morning Herald*, 8 Oct. 1983.

39 "7-0, Spartans Romp." *The Durham Sun*, 8 Oct. 1983.

40 Featherston, Al. "Spartans Post Perfect Record." *The Durham Sun*, 4 Nov. 1983.

41 Featherston, Al. "Spartans Post Perfect Record." *The Durham Sun*, 4 Nov. 1983.

42 Carson, Al. "Playoffs: Southern Facing Potent Wishbone." *The Durham Sun*, 11 Nov. 1983.

43 Featherston, Al. "Spartans Post Perfect Record." *The Durham Sun*, 4 Nov. 1983.

44 Chandler, Charles. "Southern Falls From Playoffs In 16-14 Loss." *The Durham Morning Herald*, 12 Nov. 1983.

45 Chandler, Charles. "Southern Falls From Playoffs In 16-14 Loss." *The Durham Morning Herald*, 12 Nov. 1983.

46 Featherston, Al. "Clinton Capitalizes on Southern Miscues." *The Durham Sun*, 12 Nov. 1983.

47 "Southern School of Energy and Sustainability." *SchoolDigger*, www. schooldigger.com/go/NC/schools/0126000550/school. aspx#:~:text=Compare%20Details%20Racial%20makeup%20 is,the%20Durham%20Public%20Schools%20District .

48 Jensen, Izzy. "A Brief Racial History of Durham." *The Standard*, 11 Apr. 2015, getthestandard.com/scoop/a-brief-racial-history-of-durham/.

49 Butchireddygari, Likhitha. "Part 1: How Durham Public Schools Became Resegregated." *Medium*, A Path Forward for Durham's Segregated Schools, 22 Apr. 2019, medium.com/race-and-equity-in-durham-public-schools/part-1-how-durham-public-schools-became-resegregated-550a0b19ad8a.

50 Southern High School. *Le Sabre, 1985*, p. 6.

51 "Southern High Tailback Is Top N.C. Football Player." *The Durham Morning Herald*, 3 Jan. 1984.